ADVANCE PRAISE FOR *The Water Calls*

"A remarkable woman with a remarkable life! I am so grateful to have been allowed access to Ariana's history, art, and guided exercises, as *The Water Calls* takes us on a gentle journey inside ourselves and reawakens our beautiful connection to Mother Earth and all her creatures. The first layer of Ariana's story and wisdom is refreshingly simple and direct ... and then, after a time, there comes a moment when we notice that all along it was weaving circular webs into our very being, slowly and powerfully absorbed like a soft spring rain, until by the end we are saturated and utterly transformed. A book to savor slowly and then read again and again."

~Amy Ricafrente, Owner of Amy's Kitchen

"Emma's journey is a tapestry of wisdom-rich stories and poems beautifully woven into the reflection of Ariana's life. Through the eyes of nature—horses, birds, coyotes, and more—Ariana was guided to uncover aspects of her life through the magic of animal wisdom. As I read this book, I laughed and I cried. I saw humanity through a new lens. Ariana is a teacher, guide, and mentor to all, and the sharing of her most vulnerable Self touched my heart with love."

~Kami Guildner, author of *Firedancer: Your Spiral Journey to a Life of Passion and Purpose*, kamiguildner.com

"Ariana's stories are private treasures that don't reveal themselves to the voyeur; rather, they are a feast for the famished *feminine* soul. It feels as if each word was set free from the magic place in between worlds, instinctively and vividly reminding us of who we really are and have always been. *The Water Calls* takes us on a journey that is utterly vulnerable and exquisitely powerful, leaving us hopeful, *heartful*, and head over heels in love with Mother Nature and all her creatures!"

~Maryanne Comoroto, I

"Ariana Strozzi Mazzucchi has beautifully crafted a must-read tale for every woman on a spiritual journey. Through her trials and tribulations, she shares how her animal guides, her sacred relationship with horses, and the healing lessons gleaned from nature helped heal old wounds and betrayals. At the end of each chapter, she offers reflections and time in nature prompts, revealing the inner workings of how a modern-day spiritual warrior finds her way back to her shamanic way of being in this world. This book is a recommended read for any intuitive, highly empathic, and earthbound being in transition."

~Kathy Pike, Author of *Life Lessons from the Heart of Horses,*
Horse Spirits Speak, and *Hope from the Heart of Horses*

"In *The Water Calls,* Emma's inspiring hero's journey offers hope and healing. Emma's pain and vulnerability are palpable, her resilience inspiring. Her story, so artfully written and vivid, was as if I were floating above, observing her struggle. Ariana demonstrates the process of self-reflection and the benefits of reinterpreting the past and reimagining the future. She gives us the template, showing by example. By following the brilliant inquiries and nature contemplations, the reader is guided by Ariana on their own journey of reconnecting to their spirit self and to the natural world."

~Hallie Bigliardi, Author of *Take Back the Reins: The Truth*
About Why You're Stuck and How to Get Moving Again

"Pagan Priestess. Healer. Wise Woman. Equine Guru. Arianna Mazzucchi leads us, with animal guides and a Northern California coastal path of watery tributaries, through the terrain of her own heartbreaking, yet triumphant journey. The path leads home to a self that is grounded in the abundance of the natural world and her own very particular exquisitely attuned relationship to it."

~Bonnie Saland, Psychoanalyst, Principal, Philomela Textiles

"Ariana gives language and creates pictures that encapsulate the precious bonds between the inner world of humans with the vibrantly alive natural world. As a woman who also has experienced a painful and traumatic marriage and divorce, I applaud her tenacity to not diminish her experience in order to appease others, but to honor it in a way that liberates the decades of silencing and diminishing women."

~Tracy Gray, Author of *Women Who Walk with Horses: Healing Through Horse Wisdom*

"An unapologetic telling of a woman's journey from innocent youth to wise woman, every page contains gems and insights that will linger long after the reader has closed the cover. With her trademark organic style— her artwork, poetry, vulnerable storytelling, and heart-centered reflections—Ariana's invitation for self-inquiry flows naturally and reads easily. Part autobiography, part self-development journal, the reflections offered at the end of each chapter will no doubt stimulate constructive contemplation."

~Kansas Carradine, Professional Trick Rider, Cavalia

"Ariana's memoir offers deeply personal insights, using nature as a teacher and the wisdom of the horses she has known and loved, along with some starkly honest memories from her past. She gives us resources to help open that doorway to our own healing. Honest, inspiring, and insightful. Thank you, Ariana!"

~Peggy Berryhill, KGUA radio

THE
Water
CALLS

THE

Water
CALLS

ARIANA STROZZI MAZZUCCHI

MERRY DISSONANCE PRESS   CASTLE ROCK, COLORADO

The Water Calls: One Woman's Journey to Reclaim Her Dignity and Freedom
Published by Merry Dissonance Press
Castle Rock, CO

FIRST EDITION 2022

Publisher's Cataloging-in-Publication data

Names: Mazzucchi, Ariana Strozzi, author.
Title: The water calls : one woman's journey to reclaim her
dignity and freedom / Ariana Strozzi Mazzucchi.
Description: Castle Rock, CO: Merry Dissonance Press, LLC
Identifiers: ISBN: 978-1-939919-64-9
Subjects: LCSH Mazzucchi, Ariana Strozzi. | Self-actualization (Psychology). |
Conduct of life. | Self-realization in women. | Self help. | BISAC BODY, MIND &
SPIRIT / Inspiration & Personal Growth | BIOGRAPHY & AUTOBIOGRAPHY /
Women | SELF-HELP / Personal Growth / General
Classification: LCC BL625.7 .M39 2022 | DDC 204/.4082--dc23

ISBN 978-1-939919-64-9

Book Interior and Cover Design © 2022
Interior Art by Ariana Strozzi Mazzucchi
Cover Design by Victoria Wolf, wolfdesignandmarketing.com
Book Design by Victoria Wolf, wolfdesignandmarketing.com
Editing by Donna Mazzitelli, writingwithdonna.com

Author has made a good-faith effort to convey the truth and essence of what
occurred in her life; however, certain names have been changed and events
have been compressed. Dialogue, especially in scenes from the distant past,
is a representation of what was spoken based on the author's recollections.

To the free-spirited women and men
I have known who taught me
to be true to myself,
to be wild of heart and spirit,
to cherish those I love,
and to ride life with passion.
And most importantly,
to my children and grandchildren.
May you always be free.

Tell me your story, and I will tell you mine.

CONTENTS

FOREWORD

THROUGH AN UNUSUAL SET of circumstances, I had a rare opportunity to spend weekends on Ariana's ranch for one entire year. During that time, I learned the names and personalities of many of her horses, witnessed the miracles of lambing season, and watched a year's worth of students transform themselves through her equine-guided education program.

Living through a full cycle of seasons at the ranch brought me so close to the natural world I could almost hear the earth breathing. It also gave me a chance to observe the life and work of a woman I had admired, both personally and professionally, for nearly three decades.

But it wasn't until she handed me this book to edit that I began to understand what I had been trying to figure out about Ariana all along: her life is like a river, flowing effortlessly between human and animal worlds. She has the natural gift of an unspoken language that transcends and includes all species. And she carries a deep intention to heal wounded humans—and a wounded planet—by bringing them together in humble, harmonic ways.

Ariana is an imaginative and evocative writer who uses stories, dreams, drawings, and poems to weave a poignant and powerful tale of personal transformation. In my work as a writing coach and mentor, I teach my students that the most intimate, relatable writing comes from an authentic, open, vulnerable place. Working around the big wooden table in Ariana's aromatic kitchen, I found her storytelling to be natural, honest, and true to the bone. Not only does she offer her own life lessons in service to others, but she suggests nature-based practices at the end of each chapter to enlighten and enrich the lives of her readers.

One thing that delights me most about this book is the magical cast of characters that accompanies Ariana on her journey. Ravens, lambs, coyotes, falcons, wind, trees, waters, and of course, horses—always, always horses—play important roles in guiding her to her full self. Parts of the story read like fables or fairytales. Others carry the indigenous wisdom of land and animals as they nudge—and sometimes push—her to embrace her true essence courageously and save her own life.

The stories in this book remind me of how connected we all are to the natural world. In my twenty years as a wilderness rites-of-passage guide, I've witnessed time and again the subtle power of nature to heal, transform, and guide. Part of Ariana's deep purpose is to help mend broken bonds between humans and nature. This book reminds us that we are never alone.

After thirty years, I now honestly know who Ariana is. Although she is an incredibly accomplished woman, her true essence is not something you'll find described on her website or spelled out on her resume. It's not something you'll recognize in her face or notice in a gesture. It's something that can only be learned from a personal story with the potential for healing others. Heartbreaking and heroic, tense and triumphant—this is that story.

Susan Hagen
Writing coach, wilderness rites-of-passage guide, and co-author of
Women at Ground Zero: Stories of Courage and Compassion

PREFACE

began journaling in 2004 to save my life. At the time, I didn't know I
needed saving. To the outside observer, my life looked perfect. I was a
successful entrepreneur, artist, and professional equestrian. I prided
myself on being a good wife and mother of three beautiful children.
In 1989, I became one of the pioneers of the horses healing humans
discourse, commonly known as equine-assisted therapy.

As a young entrepreneur, quickly seeing the link between embodied leadership and the art of horsemanship, I founded Leadership &
Horses™, which grew to become known as equine-guided education and
coaching. In 1994, I created a profitable institute in embodied leadership
to provide my then-husband with his legacy dream and a business that
would support my children and me.

My family and career were flourishing. However, behind the scenes,
my life was unraveling at the seams. Refusing to see it, I worked smarter,
tried harder, and avoided looking in the mirror to see why my interior life
was in shambles. Somehow, I'd lost my way. I'd become disconnected from
my spirit self—the true core of who I was born to be in the world. And I
had no one to talk to.

My husband and I lived a high-profile life in a small but powerful niche market of self-development. The gossip channels ran deep. Besides, of all people, we were supposed to have it all together. I didn't want to share my feelings with anyone because I was afraid that people would think I was crazy. Everything looked perfect on the outside, just the way I had intended it to be.

Yet, my intuition was screaming that if I did not pay attention to what was happening within, my life was at stake. My instinct sent me to pen and paper, but I had no words to explain my feelings. So I began drawing illustrations of a woman and a horse. I felt grounded when I was drawing, and my life made sense. Illustrations led to journaling and writing poems. They were a way to go within and let my intuition speak to me.

While journaling, I disguised myself as "Emma" so no one would know I was writing about myself. Writing Emma's stories gave me a whole new level of creative freedom I hadn't expected. I excitedly allowed the animals to dialogue with Emma, which was common in my private life. As my stories and poems grew, I noticed that they resonated with the illustrations I drew.

As I continued to lose my grip in the human world, my animal friends called me back to the essence of my childhood and the lessons I learned from my early life in nature. My deep connection to the natural world was a safe place to reconnect to myself. My intuitive self knew this, although my rational mind resisted. A big part of me didn't want to admit I was under serious duress. I was fighting for my dignity, and I was losing the battle. I didn't know this in a cognitive way; I couldn't speak to it directly. But my intuitive self knew I needed to return to my private world in nature to re-find myself. In this world, I was understood, and I was respected.

Initially, the horses of my childhood came to me, and then the land and the waters near where I grew up. Golda was the first horse to visit with her invisible ghostly presence, offering me a haunting message I didn't want to hear. Each animal in this book gave a cookie crumb to guide me toward answering the most important questions of my life: "How can I reconnect to my true self? How can I find the courage to take a stand for myself in the human world? How will I reclaim my freedom and power?"

The journey that ensued was arduous and extremely painful. It was also an intensely rich time of coming home to my original self—my spirit self who has guided me through most of my life. She is the one I had abandoned to not make others feel uncomfortable. I realized that I had sent her underground because I didn't feel safe to be truly myself in the human world.

My journey to come back into my own skin, as depicted in these stories, poems, and drawings, has been vital not only to my existence but to the work I am destined to bring forward in the world. I have no regrets about any part of this journey.

Like any artist, the process of shedding one's skin to reveal the inner experience is both enlivening and terrifying. It is exhausting and enriching all at the same time. It is vulnerable. And, in the end, it is simply an expression of love: for life, for the gifts given and received, for finding that one is never truly alone.

As I go forward in my life, this I know: Mother Nature is always beckoning. She is always ready to welcome me home again. She is ready and waiting for you too.

Ariana Strozzi Mazzucchi
October 1, 2021

IN BETWEEN THE WORLDS

I grew up "in between the worlds." My early life experiences with horses, combined with time in nature with my best friends—animals, plants, trees, moss, and rocks—taught me a form of communication I trusted and relied upon. On the other hand, the world of human beings was confusing to me. I felt like I was in a foreign land, and I didn't understand the language.

When I was a little girl, I didn't know that I was dyslexic, yet I didn't feel like the other kids. I didn't track in words spoken; I felt my way through each day. My mom tried to teach me how to read with a giant red book that was practically bigger than me. It was useless. Words made no sense, even when written. I mixed dressage terms like a *piaffe* and a *passage* because they both started with a *p* and had an *a*. I didn't want anyone to know I was not tracking the spoken word. Like an animal, I learned early on to listen to people's energy. I didn't know I was doing that, but it was how I made sense of things. The way horses and animals responded to the people in my life affirmed this secret language—the energy of communication, not the words of humans.

I was told that animals don't speak, feel, or have emotions. I could not believe the words my elders said, so I grew up keeping my animal ways a secret.

I often interpreted things differently than others, leading to a further sense of separation from people. I wasn't like the other kids. I was extremely sensitive to other people's energy, but it seemed like no one else saw what I was seeing.

For instance, it bothered me when kids teased Mia, who was overweight, so I made friends with her. I noticed that my riding teacher would get so stressed out before a horse show, her horse would go lame the day before the event. I knew he was taking on her stress. Nobody else saw those patterns. So, I kept my impressions to myself, thinking there was something wrong with me.

I was raised to be practical, logical, and unsentimental. Dinner was at 6:00 p.m. every evening. And each night, before we could eat, my mother made sure we had our napkins in our laps and our silverware in the right place. At the dinner table, when I talked about my day with the horses, my father would often say jokingly, "Well, if we are ever poor, we can eat your horse for dinner." The best part of my life was likened to a piece of meat.

In kindergarten, I crossed out the lips of anyone smiling, including myself, in my class photo. I still have it and always wondered why I did that. I realized as I was journaling that I was mad at my mother at the time because she cut my hair. My hair was part of my wild mane. Cutting my hair felt like purposeful humiliation.

My parents often had dinner parties for my father's students and colleagues. My mother was a great hostess, and she taught me how to be a great hostess too. I was raised to have my house, manners, and dining table always ready and in proper form in case "the queen" came to dinner. My mother would say condescendingly to me after I polished all the silver before a dinner party, "What if the queen comes to dinner? Do you think this is good enough?" The unspoken answer was, "It was never good enough." I was proud of my work, but my mother could not be pleased.

I did enjoy the evenings when guests were over. During that time, our home felt like a happy, welcoming place. I liked making the food, preparing the flower arrangements, and greeting the guests at the door. I liked serving people at the parties and especially enjoyed the smiles on their faces as I offered them hors d'oeuvres. I enjoyed my father's colleagues and their wives. I learned a lot from them as I listened to their conversations. I much preferred to be a fly on the wall listening to their amazing accomplishments and intellectual banter than playing with the other kids.

Other happy times in our family were when my father took us camping or fishing. Spending time in my father's office painting or paying the bills (yes, I even paid the bills) was like a quiet meditation, during which I didn't have to feel the pain in the main house. I could escape into my own fantasy world.

But I had to wonder: Was spending time with my father really an escape or a reprieve from the rest of our home life? As a child, when I asked my dad what he thought of my paintings, he would offer his artistic criticism, pointing out the ways my artwork could be improved upon. I always took his feedback as fatherly love, never considering that I didn't receive the one thing kids want most: words of praise such as, "Wow, great job, honey!"

There was no hugging or affection in my house. No touch. Thank goodness I could hug the animals and my little brothers. My ex-husband used to say I wasn't a good hugger and teased me for it. I didn't like teasing. I still don't. But by that time in my adult life, I was used to being criticized and put down for who I was. It was just the way things were—I was never good enough.

Like water off a duck's back, I thought I had learned to handle the shaming and had somehow risen above it like the horses had taught me.

Even though I was upset when I was in the midst of conflict with another person, I tried to follow what my father always said (with no emotion): "Turn the other cheek."

At some point, though, I challenged this idea. "Why turn the other cheek? Just to be slapped again? That no longer makes sense to me." On the one hand, I understood the concept, "Raise your consciousness above the inequities in this world; see things unemotionally." On the other hand, however, I heard myself asking, "How many slaps and now punches to the face do I need to tolerate before I can say enough is enough?"

Even though I wasn't being physically beaten or sexually abused in my marriage like some of my friends experienced, something else was wrong. I felt like I was under attack and fighting for my life. Not my physical form, but my spirit, my original self, who I am. I was in an invisible warzone, and I only had myself to rely on.

No one looking in from the outside understood. Everything looked fine on the surface. We weren't poor. We weren't homeless. We had a thriving business. We had an intact family. So why should I complain?

Through the process of journaling, I came to see a pattern in my life that I call psycho-spiritual abuse. To me, this kind of abuse takes place when another person attacks your spirit or tries to take your essence, your original self.

My mother was one of the first people in my life to squash my spirit. My father often said he would come home, and she and I would be on opposite sides of their bed crying. I have an image ingrained in my mind of me as a little girl sitting on the floor crying. My face is turned upwards, and my arms are outstretched. I'm asking to be picked up. But no one comes to my rescue.

My mother was prone to severe depression and often stayed in her room for days, expecting me to feed her and bring her tea. When she was up and about, she would get angry at me for no reason. She was like Jekyll and Hyde. I could feel her anger and wrath through all the cells in my body. I would get so scared I felt like my body would turn into liquid and lose its structure, like water spilling from a broken glass.

I couldn't understand why she said so many mean things to me that weren't true. My thoughts ingrained in memory went something like this: *I can't see why she is saying such a mean thing to me. It's not true. I'm nothing like that. But she's my mom, so she must be right.*

The only way to get away from her tyranny was to agree with whatever she said, which created a vicious cycle: I gave in to her reality and abandoned my own. She wasn't happy until I repeated her untruths about me. So I learned early to shame myself.

I saw this pattern all too well in my adult life. Someone could say something untrue to me or about me, and I listened. I doubted myself, thinking they were right. I have finally learned another response: the other person's interpretations are simply theirs. Their accusations are not truths. Their assessments of me are not my truth. And I don't have to fight to be seen for who I truly am anymore.

As I dove deeper into my journal, looking into my past, trying to understand why my life was falling apart, I saw this pattern repeated in my relationships with men. I unconsciously recreated this same scenario, letting someone destroy my self-dignity and treat me with disrespect. I would try to fight for my dignity but ultimately felt there was no way to win. My only way out of these psycho-spiritual attacks was to give in, to give away my self-respect. I let them take my spirit and squash it in their clenched fists. When they finally saw me submit to them, they would turn away with a smile on their face. They knew they had won by defeating me. That is precisely what they wanted. I was left alone in shame once again.

My mother was intuitive, but I think that part of her was punished as a little girl. Being sensitive and being a feeling person didn't fit into her father's strict navy household. This duality of self—feeling woman versus proper woman—passed down to me. I felt her battle wounds, but no one spoke of them. They lived under the floorboards of our house. No one spoke about the elephant in the room.

My mother's father was a rear admiral in the navy and was stationed in Pearl Harbor when my mother was little. When she was four years old, she spent four days in a bomb shelter under the ground with her mother, other children, and their mothers. I can only imagine how terrified she and all of the others must have been in that cement box hearing the bombs. I'm certain she witnessed the tragedy of hundreds of families in their village, along with her father and all the other men who survived and experienced trauma in response to so many lives lost right before their eyes, not being able to save their brother soldiers or their sons.

When I was a little girl, my father coined post-traumatic stress disorder. Although this is one of the most significant accomplishments of his life, which has helped millions of people worldwide, he could not heal his wife's trauma.

I was my mother's first child and had no idea how to save her. So, without knowing what else to do, I took her burden on as my own. I became a little mother for my mother and brothers. My friends didn't like to come over to play because I was too busy taking care of my brothers, doing the laundry, or making dinner. I wanted to help her; I wanted her to be happy. My efforts were never good enough, though. So, I tried harder. I tried to be the solver, the fixer, the rescuer. I could rescue baby birds, heal wounded animals, but I could not rescue my mom.

Burned in my memory are numerous visual snapshots of my mother sitting in a chair with a void look on her face, her lips turned down in a deep frown. Her deep sadness permeated the room like a wet rag over your face. It wasn't until I was teaching an equine- therapy program in 2019 that I had an "aha" moment. Some of the participants were veterans that had overcome PTSD and wanted to help other veterans and first responders recover from trauma. My son had recently joined the marines, my father had coined PTSD, and I was helping veterans overcome PTSD with equine therapy. For the first time, I saw this convergence of PTSD in my family tree. It was like a drive-in movie screen with the giant screen saying, "Do you get it now?"

All of a sudden, my reality changed. I had compassion for my mother in a new way. I realized that snapshot of my adult mother sitting in a chair, with a blank stare on her face, was her little four-year-old self trying to survive in the bomb shelter. Her body was stuck in that traumatic time in her life. Despite her numerous accomplishments as a physical therapist, despite having a good husband and good kids, she was lost in indescribable pain.

Coming to these realizations, I could begin to journey more consciously to heal the ancestral wounds that riddle my family. Through my soul-searching journey into the intuitive flow of my unconsciousness, I finally came to see much of the ancestral wounding that has haunted my family and me for generations. Until I allowed myself to go into my past and see it through the ancient reflections of water, I carried around post-traumatic wounds that were not mine.

By writing through Emma's eyes, I was able to take a bird's eye view to see how my early years were shaped emotionally through the invisible field of my energetic surroundings. After spending too much time contemplating, "What is wrong with ME?" I started to morph into, "What family patterns can I change in my lifetime so my children can have a different story?"

In my writing, I tried to focus on my perceptions and "felt experiences" because I know deep down inside that only I can change my trajectory. I searched for the stories I created about myself in relation to other people. I documented the stories others told me about who I was and was not. I searched for the places where I had taken on the burdens of others as if I was the one responsible for their happiness.

I started to see a thread between the animal characters in my book and emotional aspects of myself. The animals, the weather, and even my own children gave me nuggets of inspiration. I had been stuck between the sensate animate world and the world of humans. I identified with the enslaved horses I grew up with. I wondered what my life as a woman and the lives of my horses had in common. I saw myself mired in a tug of war between being dominated and subordinated or fighting for my life. Like an either–or world, I would either win or lose. I wanted to shift from being a victim to being a free spirit who had the power to shapeshift my wounds into freedom and choice.

Writing *The Water Calls* is how I finally said no to other people's assessments and took a stand for who I really am, without apology. I have spent my whole life navigating between the logical rules of humans and the sensate, non-linear wisdom of the natural world. This book is about my quest to build a bridge between my animalness and the human world as a way to reclaim my dignity.

Before I wrote *The Water Calls*, I thought I had pretty much figured out who I was, how I got conditioned by my life's experiences, and how to control my responses to life's ups and downs. Journaling in the third person about my life experience, woven with the metaphors from the natural world that mirrored my intuitive interior landscape, helped me unravel the bandages I had wrapped around my wounded heart.

The animal-plant world is honest, authentic, sensate, and clear-minded. It has always been my true home and where I feel emotionally and spiritually safe. My animal friends gave me courage and strength as the messengers of my spirit self to set myself free.

I am the heroine of my own story. I am a wild woman, never to be tamed. I am Ariana. I stand tall, without apology or shame.

MY INVITATION TO YOU

In my professional life as a healer and leadership coach, I help set people free to be who they are meant to be. Along with the horses, I cut the energetic cords of entanglements that limit people's sense of value and interior dignity.

Many of the people I work with are highly successful on the outside tapestry of their life. But inside, they suffer from "not being good enough," "not being worthy enough," "being too much," and a myriad of other shaming beliefs. Mother Nature doesn't shame you. I believe that listening to your animal body will give you the tools to set yourself free from the tyranny of shame.

I have heard thousands of stories of deep traumas, wounded psyches, disrespectful acts, and massive miscommunications. Everyone has a wound, a painful experience that gets remembered in the sinew of the flesh. Our animal bodies remember all our life experiences—the good, the bad, and the ugly.

Imagine your body as your animal self, your true self. Your body is the first responder and primary informant. It responds to the energetic tone of the environment and to other people's energy via subtle, unconscious, yet remembered sights, sounds, smells, and other visceral stimuli, such as a person's tone of voice or the tension in a person's eyes. Your mind comes along after the fact and makes up an interpretation of what happened. These stories are literally made up. They may even have been given to you or told to you by someone else. Our culture is trained to rely only on these stories, our mind's attempt to control our experience. Yet, this is often where trouble starts.

What stories about who you are—and who you are not—have you taken on as your truths? Perhaps a parent, teacher, or friend told you their interpretation, spoke it as truth, and thus, you took it on as truth. Or perhaps you inherited values that got passed down on silent trails of tears or even blood memory.

The Water Calls is about how I learned to set myself free. I share my personal story with you as an invitation to explore your own journey and set yourself free from other people's expectations and assessments. Within each chapter, I share the poetry I wrote as I sought to make sense of my experiences. These poems were a different way to access my intuition and inner feelings. They are presented in their "pure" state—spontaneous, intuitive spurts that often came before the journaling of Emma's journey. I invite you to allow your truths and insights to flow through you spontaneously as well.

At the end of each chapter, I offer opportunities for reflections and contemplations with nature as your guide. Express, explore, imagine, challenge, and create. If an exercise resonates with you, go ahead and give it a try. Dive into your authentic expression with complete abandon and without apology. This is a place you do not need to protect anyone but yourself.

Allow yourself to draw, reflect, write, make up stories, and simply ramble. Delight in the inarticulate. Disallow comparison and critical perceptions.

Give yourself permission to write *your* story. The art of writing as a form of self-reflection has no rules. It is not governed by anyone but you.

Stay in the present, go into the past, explore the future, or all the above. Invite new possibilities and stories to unfold naturally.

If you'd like, you can color in the illustrations. They may also inspire you to draw or create art in other forms.

There is no right way to write, draw, or explore the natural world. If you find that self-judgments are stopping you from free expression, write them down, give them a name, create their character, or draw a picture of them. You can give them space in your journal, but don't let them stop you.

You'll notice that the animal characters—even the weather and grasses—are strong and wise. They are authentic. They carry wisdom. They don't care what others think of them. By exploring their energy and presence as a direct metaphor of my personal experience, I allowed them to guide me out of the rational prison that comes with being a human being. This, too, is your opportunity.

If you resonate with specific animals, plants, flowers, or even fairies or angels, give them a voice. Describe or draw their presence. Who do they want you to be? What do they want to tell you? Focusing on the energy of their presence—and your energy in response—can help you uncover the essence of stories that are no longer serving you. You can then create new stories, new interpretations of who you are now and who you are becoming.

As you write, draw, and spend time in nature, let go of shame, blame, and guilt. Set your spirit free to be all that is not defined by human's narrow-minded scope. Does the rock judge you? Does the tree shame you into feeling bad about yourself? Does the rain blame you? No. Write down the ugly, write down the beautiful, write down the old, and call in the new.

The chapter "Spirit Horse Returns" was the first story I wrote. It was the beginning of my process of going within to try and understand, through my own intuitive and artistic process, what was no longer working in my life. For a few years, I thought I would never be able to write the truth about my marriage because I was worried about the impact it would have on my ex-husband. I waited. And then one day, I *had to* write it. I had to explain why Emma was in so much pain. It was also the confession I needed to make to set myself free.

For many years, I wasn't sure when and if I would ever find my new story. It has taken me fourteen years to complete *The Water Calls*. Now that it is complete, I am free to write my new story. I offer these reflections to assure you that your journaling does not have to be a sequential process. Allow yourself to write whatever you feel like writing.

I use several stories and poems from this book in my real-life teaching. For example, I read the story about Golda, the spirit horse, to draw out the question for my students, "Where are you stuck in your stall?" and "How do you get out of the stall where you have confined yourself?" The chapter "The Gully" is another great teaching story to encourage participants to explore their own demons hidden in the gullies of their minds.

The power of storytelling is ancient. It is a primordial desire to explore our interconnectedness, the deeper meaning of our lives, inner intentions, and dreams. Storytelling brings us closer to our loved ones and the universal magic of balance, forgiveness, possibility, love, and hope. When we allow ourselves the freedom to share our stories, we empower others to do the same. This is what I hope my stories will do for you.

This is a deeply personal book that was never intended for the public eye. Years after writing it, though, I realized my process could be helpful to others seeking answers to deep questions in their lives. My hope is you will be inspired to take the reins in your own hands, set yourself free, and ride your spirit horse through your life, never to be tamed by other people's stories about who you are and who you are not.

Navigating between the logic of our mental acumen and the numinous underbelly of our imagination is this journey called Life. It is both our opportunity and our challenge. Love allows forgiveness, which means "to give." The only person in the world you need to love is yourself. You are the only one who can set yourself free.

I look forward to hearing (in the silent airstream of consciousness) your new story, freedom, insights, and opportunities. I invite you to begin the healing journey to set your spirit self free.

The Estero Beckons

Emma was born knowing who she was; yet, she often felt an overwhelming sense of loss. She couldn't figure out the reason for this loneliness until the world she had created crumbled at her feet despite all her attempts to hold it together. She felt like an unmoored boat drifting at sea. She had no idea how she got there or how to get back to shore.

Whenever Emma needed to find herself, she went to the ocean. She loved the ocean and all its mystery. It was the place where Emma always remembered who she was. It was the place she needed no name—a place where she made no excuses. Her sadness disappeared. Her lightness of being was free, like the ocean, never to be tamed.

As a girl, Emma rode her horse on the beach every day. Sometimes she brought her friends; hoping they could catch a glimpse of her real self in the water. Perhaps they could feel her, understand her, and accept her if they breathed the same air she did, felt the same salty wind on their faces.

As a woman, Emma knew the ocean would help her find her way. There was still hope. She was not lost at sea for all of eternity. The ocean called her back home to the waters of her beginning.

One morning, while the kids were still in school, Emma hitched her trailer, loaded up her bay and white mare, Lacey, and headed to the coast. It was quiet on the beach; the waters glistened, and the waves quietly pushed shells to shore. Emma jumped on Lacey's bare back and headed down the beach. The sand crunched under Lacey's hooves in melodic rhythm.

"Where did I go wrong? What did I miss? I must have missed something," she pondered, finding no answers in sight.

"Oh, shush already. Look at the waves with me." Lacey threw her head and looked out to sea.

"All right already, let's go for a run." Emma leaned forward, and off they went.

They galloped along the shores, running away from the chaos and stress of the human world. Their manes danced in the salt-scented air. As if by magic, the most beautiful wave formed in front of them. Its white mane danced on tall turquoise waves while the shorebirds flew just above the surface of the hidden waters in front of them. She couldn't help but laugh with pure delight.

The wave carried her back to her childhood. It was a time of solitude in human form, but one of togetherness in the natural world of her animal brothers and sisters. She took in the salty air and imagined herself as a mermaid swimming with the seals, popping up for air, looking at the people on the shore, wondering who they were, and then slipping back under the surface of the blue waves to hide once again.

Lacey and Emma stepped into the ocean and rode alongside the wave. She saw her destiny—a destiny filled with a past, a present, and a future. She could see all of it, feel all of it. And yet, she knew—and was at peace with knowing—she would never be able to share this part of herself with anyone fully, and that sometimes, great loneliness would follow.

Emma remembered the shores where she grew up—Tennessee Valley, Stinson, Bolinas, and Muir Beach. As a girl, she walked along the estuaries on foot or atop her mare to get to the ocean. For thousands of years, humans lived in balance with the unique fish, birds, and plants that shared the transitional waters where salt water and fresh water mixed. Everyone swam together, and there were no borders.

The estero *is* the meeting place of the gods. *She is* the place where fresh water and salt water meet and mingle. Without her, there is no life, no transition from land to sea. She is the meeting place for the fisherman and the mermaid, the girl and the seal. She is a place to rest for weary shorebirds. Each year, she waits for the salmon to swim upriver to lay their eggs—the salmon that will someday feed the two-legged man and the four-legged bear. She offers sandy shores for seals to breed, rest, and frolic. She provides the mouth of transportation for man and all his industrial undertakings. Without her, life on earth would not exist.

Her shores used to be busy and full of life. Her channels were deep and wide. She is not in balance anymore. Where are the turtles that used to sit on the logs while the tide went in and out? Where did the otters go who used to play hide and seek? Emma felt the pain of the estero and saw the veins of the estero filling with silt from erosion caused by the human's quest to dominate nature.

The humans had forgotten that her shores were where they had begun. She was no longer respected or revered. Her importance as the harbinger of imbalance fell on deaf ears.

Emma wept over the slaughter of the ancient redwood trees of Mt. Tam, now gone, deforested, leaving the raw, exposed dirt flowing like The Great Mother's blood down her curvaceous slopes and suffocating the home of the gods. San Francisco was built on the death of whole forests. No one talked about this.

Emma didn't have words to express the disrespect she witnessed and felt. The ocean reminded her that she was chosen to be an invisible bridge between the world of humans and the earthly ways. The estuary reminded her of the sacred space in between the never-ending effort to find balance itself—a balance between being domesticated and being wild, being fresh and being salt, being human and being animal.

Emma always felt the interconnectedness of all things. She knew without knowing that some beings could only survive in the fresh water, and some could only survive in the salty sea. But few beings could survive in the transition zone that the estuary provided. To do so required a different kind of resilience, a tolerance for both the salt of the sea and the freshness of inland waters.

The estero was guiding her back to her original self, the part that lived between the worlds so she could find the courage to face the biggest storm of her life.

My Blood Is Old

I am of the earth, above and below.
I am the earth breathing the same air as my animal brothers.
I am timeless, living before all there is to remember.

My blood is old
Running through my veins like water
It knows things I do not understand,
Things I do not need to know.

I am here to offer you my story
I am here to give you hope.
I will not leave my position.

I have had enough of the death and slaughter
The rape and pillage of our free spirit
The disrespect upon our Great Mother.

I am a wild animal,
My spirit is strong
Calling in the winds of freedom.
My blood is old
It remembers.

Opportunities and Contemplations

REFLECTION

Why did I so quickly find myself in my past when I went to the ocean that day? In a flash, I was back at the stomping grounds of my youth at the base of Mt. Tam and my daily journeys along the estuary and creeks. I remembered that I had always felt at peace when I was at the ocean's edge. I found hope in sad times. I felt a sense of belonging when I was feeling alone in the world of people.

Perhaps that is why the ocean took me back to a time in my life when I felt connected. I needed to go back there to re-find myself.

I knew something was terribly wrong in my life, but I couldn't figure it out. I wrote several essays before I made this connection to my watery roots. In fact, this was one of the last chapters I wrote. After years of journaling, I saw the relevance the estuary and the ocean still have in my life. The water is the common thread of my life, bringing me back to my own emotions.

In high school, I romped around Bolinas, Stinson Beach, and through the forest to Olema and Pt. Reyes in Northern California. During my last year in high school, I moved my horse to Muir Beach, where the turtles flourished along the willow-dense shores of the creek as it flowed through the valley to the sea. We rode the trails into Muir Woods, through the meadows, and over the creeks. The trails were endless.

When I left home for college, I spent many years inland, not far from the sea, but too far away, really. Perhaps that was part of the problem. I was like a turtle with no water. My energy was drying up, bit by bit, and I wasn't noticing.

This moment on the beach, experiencing that wave, took me into the memory portal to remember my solid ground. My spirit self always waits for me here. And so, as I neared the end of my marriage, I re-found my beginning, guided by nature, reminding me why I live in this world and not another. The metaphor of the estuary as the transition zone hits me deep in my being. It answers that part of me that lives between the worlds. The part of me that can mediate between others.

The estero began to call me in 2000, just after I had moved to a new ranch in Valley Ford, California. I was finally close to water again, after over twenty years. My home and barn overlooked the Estero Americano valley, a massive winding chain of streams and creeks flowing wildly and freely through private lands to find the ocean.

From my house on top of the small coastal mountaintop, I could see water in three of the four directions. Looking east, past our deck, there was a large spring-fed pond, lush with imagination, fish, and waterfowl. To the south, I could lose myself and any sense of worry looking down upon the Estero Americano as it snaked its way to the ocean. To the west, I could even view a sliver of the Pacific Ocean and smell the salty air traveling timelessly inland. It was a grand and panoramic sight.

As my heart grew sad and weary in what I perceived to be the day-to-day failures of my life, a deep loneliness prevailed. I soon began to see that the estero, the pond, and the ocean were my watery lifelines, my spiritual resource to come home to. It was as if these places and their local wildlife knew I was in trouble and were trying to get my attention, calling me home.

THE POWER OF PLACE—
Where Is Your Sacred Place, and Who Are You There?

- Reflect upon a place where you feel connected and balanced. Perhaps the forest, the river, or the sea.
  - What's the first story or image that comes to you?
  - Who were you when you were in your sacred place?
  - Do your guides visit you here?
  - What metaphor does this special place represent for you now? Like me, you can always come back to this part later.
  - Does the metaphor of a transition zone, perhaps even between reality and imagination, resonate with you? Do you want to explore it in writing or an illustration?

TIME IN NATURE CONTEMPLATION

Go to a place you like to visit. If you can find a waterway, that might be interesting because water is like a direct line to the interior intuitions and deeper emotional landscape. How is water different from rock? Share a prayer of thanks out loud to this place.

The Little Paint Mare

A s a little girl, Emma spent her days at the creek playing with water skeeters and making secret forts for herself and her spirit friends. The quiet redwood trees towered above, holding sacred space to explore and imagine. Emma's mother didn't notice that her daughter would be gone for hours. Maybe that is why she always made sure Emma had many animals in the house. Her mother knew Emma always came home to take care of them.

Although her mother was not available emotionally, she loved horses. Emma's mom came from generations of accomplished horsemen. Horses were her mother's lifeline, and somehow, she knew that Emma would need horses to keep her spirit safe from the world that was coming toward her.

Her mom started Emma on horses at the age of two. Emma had a different experience with her mother when they were around horses. Her mother smiled and laughed. Emma liked this very much.

One day, Emma heard horses whinnying nearby. She looked up from the kitchen sink and saw horses grazing on the steep hill across the creek.

She asked her parents if she could walk up the hill to see the horses. Her mom thought that was a good idea and found the lady who owned the horses. Her name was Peggy Adams, and she gave riding lessons to the local kids.

To get to her lessons, Emma crossed the creek and climbed one of the steepest hills of Mt. Tam. Each time she made her way to Peggy and her horses, the trip felt like days of climbing a steep fortress that only the brave would attempt. Under Peggy's tutelage, Emma's lifelong relationship with horses took solid ground.

Sometimes her friend Isabel would walk up the hill with her, and. They imagined they were horses, like Black Beauty and her friends. They took turns having a good owner or a bad owner.

Peggy taught Emma the basics of horsemanship. She was grounded, quiet, never ill-tempered, and had a patience about her that even Emma could not achieve. Peggy reminded Emma of her father. He was a quiet presence, even though he traveled a lot. When he was home, Emma spent as much time as she could in his studio painting or drawing. They often shared silence while she drew pictures, and he wrote his book or painted along with her.

Emma's father loved time in nature. He loved camping, fishing, and painting in nature. He often took her and her two younger brothers on weeklong camping trips. Her mother usually didn't go. Emma loved the times they had pack mules carry in their week's supply of food as they walked on foot in some of California's most pristine parklands.

Her godfather, who often accompanied them on their trips, made sourdough bread in an oven he dug out of the ground and brought fresh steak. Her father brought art supplies to draw and paint. Her father and godfather were both great fishermen. Emma loved fishing. She also loved sitting at the shore watching her father paint peaceful scenes by the stream's edge. The world seemed integrated and safe when she was with her dad and godfather in nature. She soaked up every moment by the water, with nothing more to do than paint or fish.

When Emma turned nine, she joined 4-H and moved her horse lessons to Tennessee Valley. Emma fell in love with a funny paint mare that had been all but abandoned in the pasture. Emma never saw anyone care for her.

"What are you doing, silly girl?" Emma laughed one day as the brown-and-white dappled mare stood on top of the feeding wall of what once was a hay manger for cows. "That's dangerous; you could slip and fall."

"I'm thrifty on my feet," the little mare replied, looking at Emma with a playful twinkle in her eyes.

Emma ran to get her mom to show her the silly girl. They both fell in love. Her mother begged the owner to let her buy the little paint mare. He finally said okay. Emma named her Sumi. Emma loved this free-spirited horse more than anything else in the world. Sumi was her everything.

Most of the time, Emma had to find her own way to get to the ranch where Sumi lived. She'd often walk seven miles along the estuary, then along the creek and up a country lane to get there. No one at home noticed or seemed to care where Emma was by day. After she cleaned her and her teacher's stalls and finished her dressage lessons, she'd take off the English saddle and bridle, put on a bitless hackamore, and she and Sumi would head down the deer trail. This was the best part of her day—the reward after the discipline of dressage training that was always so serious. Sumi didn't like to do dressage, but Emma insisted because it was the only way they would get to do their favorite event, the jumping!

As they rode the trail together, they were one, and they were free. Emma talked to Sumi about her life at home. She told her about the kids at school. She sang songs to the eucalyptus trees about how beautiful they were.

Each summer, Emma rode by herself from Tennessee Valley to horse shows at Fort Cronkite, Muir Beach, and the Southern Marin

Horsemen's Association in Mill Valley. Emma's favorite class was the cross country course at Fort Cronkite. The jumps were made out of tree trunks and piled-up railroad posts set out in a flat grassy area just out of view of the ocean. Some of the jumps were almost as tall as Sumi herself. Emma had to stand high in her stirrups so Sumi could reach up and over the jumps.

At the end of the day, Emma put the blue ribbons they had won on Sumi's bridle, and off they'd go. Sumi held her head high as if she were proud of her ribbons. The blue ribbons danced in the wind as the lone girl and her horse headed north, back over cow pastures and down to the valley where the stable lay.

Whenever her mom saw Emma acting too proud about her bond with Sumi, she'd say, "Remember, Emma, Sumi is my horse, not yours." This hurt Emma because she and Sumi were inseparable.

"But I'm the one who goes to the stable every day. I am the one who takes care of Sumi. She's my horse."

Her mother insisted, "No, she's mine. I paid for her."

"Mom, I'd like to buy Sumi from you," she said one day with a big smile on her face.

"No, Emma, Sumi is mine. I don't want to sell her to you."

Emma didn't understand why her mother didn't appreciate her spirit of responsibility. At her young age, she had no idea that it was her mother's way of having control over her. Emma thought that maybe her mother needed the paint mare to be a lifeline, too, and that was the reason she wouldn't sell Sumi to her. It seemed her mother would never let Emma have Sumi as her own.

Emma knew that Sumi was her horse in spirit, so it didn't matter who "owned" her. She was proud of her dedication to Sumi. Sumi was her best friend, her mother spirit, her expression of love.

After Emma's consistent pestering, her mother finally agreed to let her buy half of Sumi. So, Emma put on several bake sales and saved up enough money to purchase her half of Sumi. It was better than nothing.

Once Upon A Time

Once upon a time
There was a little paint mare
With white and chestnut hair
Even a few dapples here and there
And believe it or not,
She was the lead mare.

This little mare stood out from the crowd
Not that she was too proud,
But rather she dared to be true
And wanted everyone else to be too.

"Forget about posturing
And bossing and pretending," she said.
"Be true to yourself instead."

Because in her heart she knew
This was the only thing that would do.
For pretense and pride were too hard to hide
And always made for an unpleasant ride.

This little paint mare
Loved to go to the fair
With little blue ribbons in her hair.
Even though the other horses frowned,
She felt like a princess that had been crowned.

And lo and behold,
She was never too bold
To show her winning prance
She made every step look like a dance.

And dance she did, chasing the wind down the beach
Or sailing over a jump that others thought was out of her reach
Even the forest was a fun place to frolic
Playing hide and seek with the raven named Molic.

Never bored was she
She was too busy being free
Relishing the sun and the wind
Even the hummingbird in the tree.

When she saw other horses who were feeling sad
She'd run to them and show them how to be glad
With a kick of her hooves and a toss of her mane
She'd get them to run until they were all happy again.

Opportunities and Contemplations

REFLECTION

When I look back at my early years, I mostly remember playing by myself outside. I didn't have any real friends or a group of playmates. I am grateful my mother supported my love of horses. It was something we both shared in common, and it was the one place we connected, at least most of the time.

Finding Sumi gave me a sense of purpose and a home inside myself. I took care of her every day. She was my responsibility, and I thrived on making sure she got out of her stall to run and play. I excelled with horses in a way most other people did not. The other ladies at the stable saw my natural way with horses and hired me to take care of their horses. At the stable, I could shine my star secretly without being seen.

I couldn't understand why my mother wouldn't let me buy Sumi outright. It was like, "Here you go, little girl. Here is something you really want. Oh, but wait, you can't have her. She's mine, and I can take her away from you any time I want. I own her, and basically, that means I own you too."

As a mother myself, and an adult looking back on that time, her decision makes no sense to me. As a mother, wouldn't you want to support your daughter at something she excelled at? I know I just expressed I was grateful she supported my love of horses. She did, and she didn't. It is still difficult for me to make sense of her actions and motivations. Yet, that was the situation I found myself in during my formative years.

My unconscious mind made up a story that goes like this: "Don't trust the good things that come into your life because they can easily be taken away. Don't trust your mother because just when you think she'll be there for you, she may purposely hurt you instead. Keep your joy a secret; otherwise, your mom might take it away."

I don't remember how I knew about the horse shows. I remember my mom driving me to the stable at the crack of dawn and dropping me off. I remember how my mom taught me to braid Sumi's mane in thin little braids and then sew them into tidy little bonnets using blue yarn. Not a wisp of hair could be out of place.

The day before the shows, I cleaned my tack and gave Sumi a bath. I cleaned and ironed my show clothes before I went to bed. In the early morning, I tucked my stiff white blouse neatly into my white jodhpurs. I put on a down jacket over my old hand-me-down wool show coat to keep me warm in the misty dawn.

I'd ride miles up and over the hill to Fort Kronkite by myself, or I'd ride down Miller Avenue to the Southern Marin Horsemen's Association (which is now the Mill Valley Community Center) to go to the horse shows.

I remember getting back to the stable late in the day, feeling ravenous. I'd eat the horses' grain and any spare carrots I could find, waiting for my mom to pick me up. She was always late. Not a few minutes late, but an hour or more late.

PRE-PUBERTY

Nine to eleven years old seems to be a significant turning point for kids. I know it was for me. I was old enough to take on the responsibility of caring for a horse. I was old enough to be able to go places without an adult. I was discovering where I had natural abilities and wanted to learn more and practice those skills.

- Was there a hobby or activity you did when you were a child that made you happy?
- Were there places where your natural abilities started to be seen by you or others?

- How did you feel when you were engaged in it?
- What was the energetic tone or mood in your childhood home? Reflect on your early years from an energetic perspective.

TIME IN NATURE CONTEMPLATION

Find a tree, a big mama tree. Sit by her or near her, so she is in your view. Ask her, "Mother Tree, I remember this time in my life (explain it to her—it can be through imagery or feelings). I am curious to know if you can help me see that time more clearly."

If something comes forward—whether a new insight, more clarity, or a new place to dig deeper—journal about it.

The Mean
Girls

Emma's days were spent either at the stable with Sumi or waiting for the time to come when she could head out there. She often spent hours and sometimes whole days alone at the old ranch. It had once been a highly successful dairy, but now the ranch had been converted to a horse stable. The dairy barn had become horse stalls, hay storage, and a covered riding arena. It was frequently cold, windy, and foggy. Emma befriended the land and its inhabitants, sensing its loneliness.

In the middle of the barn, hundreds of bales of hay were stacked up high into the rafters, enough to feed the horses for several months. Emma loved to climb up the bales to the top, to get away from the outside world and daydream. In the late afternoon, the horses from the fields were brought into single chutes like the cows once had, and the cowboys would throw the flakes of hay into the mangers below.

An old house lay at the south end of the land, next to a seasonal creek. The potter who used to live there had dumped his abandoned clay pots in the field by the horse's water trough. On lonely days, Emma wandered there, picked up dry clay balls, soaked them in water, and made horse statues that she placed daintily on the windowsill of the tack room.

As Emma reached middle school age, several new girls brought their horses to be pastured at the ranch. The place where they had kept their horses had been turned into housing developments, so Tennessee Valley became their new stomping ground.

Before the other girls brought their horses to the ranch, it was only Emma and a bully of a girl named Kerry. It was often just the two of them on the ranch with their horses; the older ladies came in the morning and were gone by the time the girls were ready to ride.

Emma and Kerry were different in nature. Emma was quiet, and Kerry was loud and rough. Even though Emma didn't feel drawn to hang out with Kerry, she felt like Kerry needed someone. So after Emma's dressage work, she took the saddle off and hung out with Kerry and her bay Morgan gelding, Smiley. Sometimes the two misfits went out on the trail together and raced their horses down the tree-studded dirt road and up the far hill. Emma loved the feel of the wind rushing by, bringing tears to her eyes as the sound of Sumi's hoof beats left dust in their tracks.

Most of the time, things were uneventful. But out of the blue, things could turn dark without warning. One minute Kerry would laugh, tossing her blond hair from side to side, and in a flash, her face would turn red and a mean scowl took over her momentary joy. Whenever that happened, Emma couldn't figure out what had prompted the shift. They could be sitting on their horses talking about nothing important, and all of a sudden, Kerry would start yelling at Smiley in an angry voice for no apparent reason. Although he had been standing quietly, relaxed, and ready for the next cue, Kerry would take her long leather reins and whip Smiley, pelting his loins from side to side until he had welts scarring his glossy red coat. The violence came out of nowhere and was scary for Emma to watch.

Emma tried to defend Smiley by asking, "Kerry, why are you hitting Smiley? He hasn't even done anything wrong." Kerry walloped him with her leather reins several more times in a vicious tantrum of anger as if to show Emma that the more she tried to defend Smiley, the more Kerry would beat him.

Emma felt helpless. She said a secret prayer to hopefully spare Smiley any more pain. "Smiley, I am so sorry I cannot rescue you from her. This is not right. You are amazing and strong. Focus on Sumi and me; we are here with you. We are one, connected to the earth, and nothing else matters," she whispered. "Maybe Kerry is being abused at home, and she's taking her wrath out on you. That doesn't make it right, but you must see something I don't that allows you to stay calm during such wrath. How can you be so brave?"

Emma started to avoid Kerry, mostly so Smiley might be spared a beating. Around this time, the new girls moved their horses to the ranch. They were already a pack. Each girl personified a different female archetype. Delia was a blond, blue-eyed beauty, graceful in her movements. Rebecca was tall, brown-haired, and rather plain. Delia was the ring leader, and Rebecca was her second in command. Delia was stunning with her slim stature and long blond hair. Rebecca was a pretty brunette with big teeth and was taller than all the girls. She followed Delia wherever she went. Kerry fit right in and continued to be tough, broody, and angry at the world. Two other girls, Jennifer and Sara, came and were the youngest. They were both fragile characters who would do anything to be friends with Delia and her pack.

These girls were no picnic. They were downright mean—beautiful and mean. Their parents were some of the most well-known self-development gurus of the era, so the disconnect made no sense. Their parents lavished them with well-bred horses and nice tack.

Emma saw right away how mean the older girls were. She didn't understand why Jennifer and Sara were so appeasing. They would do anything for these mean girls. They let the older girls bully them into humiliation.

Emma didn't get involved; instead, she headed off down the trail to the sea by herself. She stayed on the outskirts of the group, partly because her tack room and horse were in another barn, partly because the mean girls were dangerous and untrustworthy, and mostly because she was not going to let them intimidate or humiliate her.

Emma was the witness. She witnessed the mean girls bullying the little girls and their horses. She witnessed the adult ladies dominating their horses with their over-controlling training methods. She witnessed animals being dominated and beaten with words, whips, and spurs. She witnessed the bigger kids at school try to get the younger kids to do drugs or have sex. She felt deep empathy for the suffering she saw around her, and yet she had no way to stop any of it.

A few more girls came to the ranch who were even older than the other girls. They bullied the mean girls, who then bullied the little girls, Jennifer and Sara. *What a mess*, Emma thought. She stayed away from the drama as much as possible and focused on training Sumi and taking care of other horses for the older ladies.

Every day after school, Emma, Delia, Rebecca, and their pack of girls took the school bus to Tam Valley and walked the last three-plus miles to the ranch. Delia and Rebecca made Jennifer and Sara carry their schoolbooks and bags of grain. These young girls carried eight to ten pounds of materials up a hill for almost four miles.

Delia and her gang made the younger girls buy cigarettes for them. They even made them steal candy at the little pharmacy at Tam Junction on the way home. They expected Emma to steal candy too.

Emma tried to tell the younger girls they didn't need to put up with such abuse, but they were lost in the illusion that if they acquiesced, they would be accepted by the mean girls. In some weird way, the twisted nature of their relationship with these older girls worked for them. Emma figured they must be living out some parallel dynamic at home. She felt the better path was to befriend the younger girls and show support and encouragement where she could.

One unusually hot summer day, the girls decided to have a water fight. It started off innocently but quickly turned mean-spirited. The older girls hosed down the younger girls and then made them roll around in the indoor riding arena, where the stall manure was dumped to soften the footing. They did this several times, laughing at the younger girls. Emma was appalled.

The pale-colored palomino mare named Golda, who had the only stall facing into the courtyard, stood witness with Emma.

"Why are those girls so mean?" she whispered into Golda's ear.

"I don't know. Why don't those little girls stand up for themselves?" Golda shook her head in sorrow. They both wanted this atrocity to stop. But Emma knew if she asked the older girls to stop, they would laugh and punish the younger girls more.

A few weeks later, after Emma had ridden Sumi and done her ranch chores, she walked up to the tack room where the mean girls hung out on their tack boxes. It was the old milk room with cement walls and floors, and it was always damp and cold. She could never figure out why they spent so much time in there, as it seemed rather like a dungeon.

As she entered the room, she heard crying coming from a tall, standing tack box made of plywood. The box was locked. The older girls had forced Sara get in the tack box, tall enough for her to stand in, and were spitting on her through the holes in the wood where branches once had been. Sara was crying and begging to get out.

Emma was so disgusted that she didn't take a moment to think. "That is not okay!" she insisted. "You let Sara out right now!"

The girls must have known that if they did not let Sara out, Emma's fiery wrath would be unleashed upon them. Without another word, Emma unlocked the box. Sara ran out of the tack room crying, tears and snot running down her face. Emma turned and left, her chest tight with anger.

The next day, Emma again headed up to the tack room. On her way, she stopped by Golda's stall and said hello to her trusted friend. As she turned to leave, several girls came rushing out of the tack room, fear in their eyes. "You better not go in there, Emma," they warned, "or Kerry will kick your ass!"

Emma could feel her blood boil. No way would she allow herself to be intimidated by this bully. She could no longer turn the other cheek. She took a deep breath and calmly walked into the tack room, turned to Kerry, who was sitting on a trunk smoking a cigarette, and firmly said, "Yes, Kerry? Did you want to talk to me?"

Kerry looked at her with hate-filled eyes.

"I heard you wanted to kick my ass," Emma said. "So here I am. Give me your best shot."

Emma was ready to fight. She wanted Kerry to hit her first so she could beat Kerry the way she beat Smiley. But Kerry must have felt Emma's determination. "I was just kidding," she said, lowering her head like it was no big deal.

That was the last time Emma bothered to go to the tack room. She stayed away from the mean girls. Later that winter, she saw Sara running out of the tack room and through the breezeway, tears streaming down her face. Sara was so frightened that she ran through mud a foot deep. She was so determined to get away that she didn't even stop when her boots, and then her socks, got sucked off by the mud. She disappeared down the road barefoot, her boots and socks left behind.

Emma never found out what had scared Sara so badly. Sara never came back. Shortly after that, the older girls got into boys and abandoned their horses at the barn. Of course, Emma didn't mind. She was too busy riding, cleaning stalls, and earning money for lessons.

Do You Know What I Mean?

Sometimes I feel so alone
The walls are red and green
Only conflict and disharmony seen
Do you know what I mean?

Living between the worlds,
The earth and trees always present, witnessing
People full of doubt and false pride
Do you know what I mean?

Is it witnessing good and evil walking down every street?
Does that make you crazy?

Like the native war pony captured by the cavalry
only to carry a rider who kills his warrior's brother.

How can this be so?
How can people be so mean?

The anger, the hurt, the pain too deep to go unseen
Do you know what I mean?

Opportunities and Contemplations

REFLECTION

This part of my early adolescence had a dramatic effect on me. It took almost fifty years for me to finally share the pain and brutality of Kerry and the mean girls. I felt helpless to stop Kerry's violent abuse of Smiley and the abuse the younger girls took.

Smiley stands out to me like a saint. His ability to withstand such abuse and somehow not be ruined inspires me to this day. As a horse trainer, I have worked with so many horses who have been ruined by abusive riders. Most horses beaten with ropes or reins go wild-eyed when you raise your hand—as if you are holding an invisible torture device, ready to unleash it on their innocent flesh. Some are beaten to an inch of their lives and lose their spirit. They become spiritually void, and you can't find them.

When Kerry was about to unleash her anger, Smiley stood there. He didn't pin his ears in anger. He didn't run away. He took the abuse. On one hand, he taught me to be resilient under such abuse. On the other hand, he showed me that no one should ever be beaten or shamed with punishing words. Yet, Smiley never seemed to lose his dignity. He didn't feel sorry for himself. He didn't lower his head and turn away from the world like some horses do.

The abuse the mean girls perpetrated on the little girls was harsh and cruel. I couldn't save them; in the same way, I couldn't save Smiley. I tried to defend them and give them options, but they were entwined in the dark ritual of abuse. I wondered what was missing in their lives. Like a lone horse, they wanted so desperately to be part of the group of girls that they allowed themselves to be dominated, to be treated disrespectfully.

As social animals, humans and horses have an innate instinct to be part of the herd or tribe. To be ostracized or excluded makes us vulnerable to predation or death. We need to belong. These younger girls were willing to be bullied so they could be part of Delia's gang.

The horses and younger girls were told who to be, how to behave, and if they didn't do what they were told, they were whipped, spurred, and ostracized. You were either on the top or on the bottom of the hierarchal chain. I tried my best to stand, do my own thing, and not get involved in the social politics.

The stable became a dark place of psycho-spiritual abuse, domination, and energetic violence. The horse owners dominated their horses into submission and made the horses dependent on them for survival. In this way, the horses had no choice but to do whatever their humans asked of them or face violent consequences. The gang of girls added to the distorted sense of order.

Even the eucalyptus trees wept daily. As a child, I could feel the historical abuse and poisoning of life, the rape of the land, the death of the redwood trees, and the soil left barren and scarred. Nothing thrived on the ranch. There was not a flower on the place. I was particularly moved by the abandoned clay pots. I wondered who the artist was and where they had gone.

When I headed out on the trail by myself, the sadness fell away. The oat grasses touched my legs as I road through the field, and I smelled sweet fragrances in the breeze, which brought a smile to my face. Even Sumi perked up, ears forward, taking faster steps until she was in a fancy jig that felt like floating on water. We were one, and the rest of the world fell away.

MEAN GIRLS AND BULLIES

- What were your junior high school days like?
- How did you respond to peer pressure?
- What did you do to fit in?
- What would you do differently now?

TIME IN NATURE CONTEMPLATION

Go outside and find a tree, a rock, a meadow, or a waterway, and ask the earth how she handles extremes. What does it mean to belong? Ask her to show you what you need to see. What needs to come to the foreground so you can untangle yourself from trying to fit in or, like in my case, being witness to dysfunction between people in your life? Offer a prayer to the earth that you will honor the past and can now release the tension that lives in your sinews. Let it all go back to the earth to be recycled into a new untangled energy for good.

The English Lady on the Flat

Emma moved her horse to Bolinas the summer before high school. Margaret, the matron of the farm, was a very tall English woman with a steep English accent who was to become like a second mother to her. The farm was forty-five minutes from Emma's home in Mill Valley. The single-lane road carved its way along Mt. Tam, winding between steep forested hills and down along the shores of the Bolinas Lagoon. Every trip to the farm was a treasure of light through redwoods, shorebirds in the lagoon, and dramatic views of Stinson Beach as the road came out of the forest.

It was too much for her mother to drive her to the farm every day, so Emma stayed at Margaret's house during the week. The Bolinas kids had to take the early bus at six-thirty in the morning so the bus could pick up Mill Valley kids later. Emma got up before dawn and washed her face with cold water because it took too long for it to get warm. Down jacket, flip flops, and dirty jeans on, out she'd go to stand on the road in the dense fog, waiting for the bus to arrive. Sometimes she couldn't even see the bus until it was right in front of her.

Once off the school bus, the Bolinas kids had to swim in the freezing cold pool to keep busy before school started. The girls wore antique, one-piece cotton bathing suits from the 1940s and rubber caps on their heads. Emma hated the suits and the cap—they were humiliating. But she didn't have a choice.

Aside from the chilly mornings and long bus ride to school, Emma loved her new routine. She made new friends, and they all had horses. After getting off the bus in the afternoon, Emma had tea with Margaret before working with Sumi. First, she'd work in the arena and then head off the beach for a run on the sandy shores. Sumi loved to splash in the waves as they traveled in and out over the wet sand. Sometimes the pelicans would fly a few waves out from them as if to join in the fun.

Emma felt confident in Bolinas. Her friends respected her and welcomed her into their pack. Amanda was tall and confident. Mira had long blond hair and surfed with the boys. Alexa, who lived next door to Margaret, didn't fit in with the other girls, but Emma made friends with her anyway.

Most of the kids surfed after school. Emma wanted to learn how to surf, but she was too embarrassed to try since the other kids were already so good. Instead, she'd ride Sumi on the shores while they surfed in the waters.

Located off the beaten path, the little town was safe for the kids to wander about on their own. It was rare to see anyone's parents around since this was "Bolinas of the 1970s." Most parents were too preoccupied with living a "hippie lifestyle"—doing drugs or having sex with each other—to offer any supervision. Emma and her friends had their routines and managed themselves.

Margaret's home felt safe. She was present, and she cared about her kids. She was consistent and reliable, unlike Emma's mother. Margaret was the epitome of the classic 1950s housewife, caring for her two children, her husband, tending the garden, and feeding the animals at dawn and dusk. She fed everyone well and provided discipline and freedom at the same time. A few months after Emma arrived, Margaret fostered two girls who were a few years younger than Emma. Kari and Penny's mother was a homeless alcoholic. Emma admired Margaret for taking care of these girls.

Margaret's husband was an award-winning film editor and traveled often. When he was home, she tended to him as if he were a king. He became the priority in the house, and everything catered around his schedule. Dinner was on time; bedtime was at eight o'clock sharp when all children needed to be upstairs and in bed. There was no time to dawdle. A few times, Emma came downstairs, not realizing how strict the rule was. Margaret and her husband were clearly having their time together and sent a most unwelcome message to any child who intruded.

Margaret was strict, but the consistency of her ongoing presence, her mothering wings enfolding and caring about where Emma was and what she was doing, worked for Emma. She liked the stability of having an elder who cared about where she was and what she was up to.

Margaret's kids were not as enthusiastic. They didn't like the ritual of eating everything on their plates. But Emma didn't mind that at all. At least there was food on her plate.

A few years went by, and life seemed as normal as a teenager's life could be. But one day, out of the blue, her mom gruffly told her she was moving Sumi to the stable in Muir Beach. Emma didn't know what had happened. All she could remember was the day her mom and Margaret had an argument, which had something to do with Emma. Margaret became gruff and distant toward Emma. Emma was shocked by Margaret's sudden unwelcoming behavior. She was abandoned by the woman she most trusted, and she didn't know why.

Emma went to Sumi's stall and wept. "What happened? What did I do wrong?"

Sumi stood quietly. After all of Emma's tears were spent, Sumi whispered, "You've got me. I'm here for you; we'll be okay as long as we are together."

On the last day at Margaret's farm, Emma said goodbye to her friends. She sneaked into the garden to eat one last tomato off the vine and said thank you to the apple tree. She rode Sumi to the cemetery and cried. She packed her tack and walked Sumi into the trailer as if they were off to a show. But they were not. They were leaving a whole way of life, an entire community of belonging.

The forty-five-minute drive over the hill seemed to take forever this final time. Emma moped in the passenger seat, unsure about how life would be from now on. Once at the Muir Beach stables, she let Sumi out of the trailer and put her in her new home on two hundred and fifty acres. Sumi quickly made her place in the herd as the lead mare. Even though she was smaller than many of the horses, she had a confidence and sureness in her presence the other horses did not. Emma smiled with pride.

The Road

The road goes in
The road goes out
The road goes in
The road goes out.

I follow the road in
Walking through fields of golden grass dried
by the heat of the sun
The tender seed heads pointing the way inward on the
quietly moving breeze
I follow, moving ever closer to the talking trees
Announcing my arrival on their whispering branches.

The road narrows, becoming a dirt path of bare earth
Passed and trespassed many times before me
The rich aromas of the pine tips fill my lungs
My heart calms, my breath deepens
I am home.

The road goes in
The road goes out
The road goes in
The road goes out.
I follow the road out

My step quickens as I move onto the once hidden path
As I leave the shelter of the trees, the breeze catches my breath
I lean into it as I walk through the golden meadow
Smelling the salty air on silent trails
The path becomes the road
The blue of the sea mixes with the blue of the sky
Grass, water, sky
Grass, water, sky.

The road ends abruptly at the cliff
Below the ocean beckons of things afar
The sky is right before me with its past, present, and future.

I could turn left toward the familiar
I could turn right toward the certainty of narrow minds
I could step off the road and jump into the unknown waters
Where perhaps the waves will take me where I am supposed
to go
My watery intuition knows the way
There are no words to say.

The road goes in
The road goes out
The road goes in
The road goes out.

Opportunities and Contemplations

REFLECTION

The contrast between my mother and Margaret was dramatic. Margaret showed me what I thought a mother was supposed to be like. I admired her, and I looked up to her. The subtle way she emotionally left me hurt me deeply. It felt like one more person I couldn't count on to be there for me.

I wondered what had caused the falling out between her and my mom. Years later, I asked my father why we had to leave Margaret's farm. He said that she and my mom had a falling out because my mom asked her to take care of me while they went to Hawaii. It was late notice and a time that didn't work for Margaret. When Margaret was done with a friend, he told me, she was done. I'm not sure of the details, and it still doesn't make complete sense to me.

Both women were raised to go to college to find a good husband. Even though they behaved differently toward their children, both embodied the way of a "good wife," putting their careers before their husband and making him the king of the house.

Margaret had a tough side to her. She wasn't a warm and fuzzy person, but she was frank and honest like a horse, and I loved her English accent. She didn't let the harshness of the world beat her down. She never complained. I liked the way it was clear she was in charge (at least until her husband came home).

EVERY WOMAN HAS THE RIGHT
to Her Own Piece of Shoreline Along the River

Like a river heading to the ocean, the evolution of the women's movement has taken several twists and turns. This is a dense and deep subject. There is no right answer to these questions. I encourage you to take some time to dig deeper into the subliminal (unspoken) messages you received related to being a woman, being a mother, being a wife. Or, if you are a man, consider what you were taught about the role of the woman, the wife, and the mother.

- Did you have a woman role model you trusted or wanted to emulate?
- What were the women of your generation like?
- What were the unspoken messages you received?
- What did it mean to be a good girl as a young woman?
- Did you compromise your free spirit to fit in or gain acceptance? If so, how?

TIME IN NATURE CONTEMPLATION

Find a place in nature where you can get quiet. Take a walk among trees or sit under a tree. What in your environment looks or feels feminine, like a "she"? What feels masculine like a "he"? Why do you think they each feel that way? Again, there is no right or wrong answer. This is simply an exercise to let nature guide you into your subconscious.

Turtle Times

Once Sumi was in Muir Beach, Emma's routine changed. After school, she drove to the stable and walked up the 250-acre pasture to find Sumi and bring her to the stable to tack her up. She felt lucky that, as in Tennessee Valley, she had her own private area at the west end of the barn by the haystack for her tack box and grooming tasks. Most of the other boarders were older career women whose children had grown up and moved away. They had fancy dressage saddles and proper equestrian attire as if going to the stable was a fashion show.

On the contrary, Emma wore jeans and her one pair of English leather boots that Margaret had given her one winter as a thank you for taking care of her filly, Penny. Emma kept to herself. She found new trails that delighted her spirit.

"Sumi, look at all the **turtles**!" Emma exclaimed as they walked along the creek that meandered to the beach. Sumi nodded her head in agreement as they bounced down the sandy trail.

Emma and Sumi were often gone for hours. First, they'd head to the beach and take a run in the deep sand as the waves crashed onto the shore. Then up the steep slope they'd go, heading south along the cliff's

43

edge. Sometimes they spent what seemed like hours looking for the end of the horizon far away over the sea and smelling the salty air as seagulls flew overhead.

"What is out there?" she asked the gulls one day as they circled and whirled with the wind.

"Forever is out there," one particularly white, healthy, feathered gull replied. "Sometimes the sea is so calm we can see the whales. But sometimes it is too scary, so we head to shore, like now."

Emma took in a few more deep breaths, and Sumi did too. A bobcat ran by, a red-tailed hawk called, and off the girl and the horse went again, running up the old fire road to get higher and higher up the hill so they could see farther and farther away. Emma didn't want to return home, but she knew she had to.

Once back at the stables, the ladies criticized Emma for riding her horse bareback and for going on such long trail rides. Their idea of a trail ride was five minutes down the road and back. They didn't know that Emma and Sumi were doing endurance training she had learned from her three-day eventing trainer when she was at Tennessee Valley. Contrary to their beliefs, she prided herself in how in shape Sumi was. She knew what she was doing and left the women to their own opinions.

One summer afternoon, Emma's mom came out to the stable with her. Her mother seemed tense and irritated. Even a ride on Sumi didn't cheer her up.

"Mom, look at the turtles in the creek," Emma pointed to three turtles resting on a log as she and her mom rode along the trail that meandered with the creek.

"Oh, yeah," her mom faintly replied. She was known as the turtle woman in the family because of her love of turtles. Her turtle collection at home even included rescued turtles. Emma was perplexed by her mother's lack of interest and enthusiasm.

Once back at the stable, they groomed their horses in silence. After putting the horses back in their field, they began the curvy drive home along Highway 1. Emma could feel her mother's tension. Her lips were pursed in an upside-down smile that was not uncommon, and her hands gripped the steering wheel. Her energy was dark and moody and filled the car with an unusual stiffness.

"What's the matter, Mom?" Emma looked at her with concerned eyes.

Her mother grimaced and tersely said, "You are lazy and irresponsible!"

Emma was stunned. "What are you talking about? I do the laundry for the whole family. I shop for meals. I make dinner every night and do the dishes, and I take care of Sumi every day."

In one short snip, her mom closed the conversation by saying, "If you are not careful, you are going to end up like your aunt. You won't amount to anything. You're just a ragamuffin after all."

Where was this coming from? What prompted such an attack? Her mom was the one who chose her clothes. Were her clothes frumpy? What was a ragamuffin anyway?

Emma knew there was no use in defending herself. She knew that any attempt she made would fail because her mother would not be happy until she won. "You must be right, Mom," Emma finally said. "I am lazy and irresponsible."

Her mother put on a satisfied look and stopped attacking her.

Emma looked out the window at the forest of bays and redwoods trilling by, as if maybe they would distract her from the deep pain she felt inside. She wanted to cry, but she didn't want her mother to win.

Emma's mom became more depressed, often not leaving her room for days. She was not well physically either. She became bedridden for six months with a back injury. The doctors told her not to get out of bed. Emma was already in charge of the family's laundry, grocery shopping, and making dinner, and now she added complete care for her mother to her daily responsibilities. She brought meals to her mom and even washed her mother's hair in bed because she was not supposed to stand up.

Every day after school, she escaped to the stable, went for a ride on the beach and through the forest, and then rushed home to take care of her mother, brothers, and dad.

The first thing she always did when she got home was check on her mom.

"How was your day?" her mother asked every day.

"It was okay," Emma replied.

"No, really, tell me about your day!" her mom insisted.

"Not much happened, Mom," Emma repeated each afternoon.

"You don't love me," her mother pouted.

Emma was confused and hurt by her mother's accusations. "What do you mean, Mom? Of course, I love you. You are my mom."

"You don't tell me what is happening in your life. You don't care about me. You don't love me!"

"Mom, how can you say this?" she asked. And on it went. This became their daily dialogue. Every day her mother was disappointed in her. Every day Emma heard, "You don't love me." She was failing to help her mother feel loved. Emma was ashamed, sad, and grew more and more resigned.

She tried harder to be a good daughter. She brought her mother gifts and told her stories, but nothing made her mother happy. Over time, her mother became angrier and angrier. Once out of bed and back on her feet, she shunned Emma.

Her mother's tirades didn't stop either. One day as Emma was doing the dishes, her mother came into the kitchen in a fury.

"I can't wait for you to move out of this house!" she yelled as she took the dinner plates out of the cupboard and, in a violent rage, threw them one by one on the kitchen floor. She was so angry!

Emma felt helpless. She didn't know what to do. She didn't understand why her mother was so unhappy, so rageful. Inside, her heart bled. Why did her mother hate her? She couldn't think of anything she had done wrong. It made no sense.

"I can't wait to move out either!" Emma retorted.

After her mother stomped out of the room, Emma bent down and picked up the broken dish pieces off the floor. A few tears streamed down her face and rested on the kitchen floor. She couldn't wait to leave. It was true.

Why?

Facing west into the ocean's fierce embrace
A brown-skinned girl sits atop a white-faced mare,
Wind pressing against their faces
Their manes stiff with longing.

Looking, searching, finding the answer
However brief.
Life is as simple as you make it
Or as difficult as the pain of birth.

Why does the wind from the sea
Carry tiny granules of salt on its breath?
Why does it push the top of the water
Push, push, push
'Til it has a white mane?

Why does the seagull dance silently in the air
Beside her asking the same question?
Why do I live in this form and not another?
Each asks the other.

A long time goes by,
Nothing happens.

And without another thought
The mare and girl
Step forward into the late afternoon sun
Heading down the deer trail to the sea
Winding their way through the bushes
Blissfully content not knowing the answer to anything.

Opportunities and Contemplations

REFLECTION

Growing up, I felt as if my mom was damaged goods, but I didn't know why. I couldn't really feel her. There was a void. It wasn't until my mid-thirties, a few years before my life started to fall apart, that I found out she was on numerous medications for depression. For goodness sake, I wish I had known. I wish someone had told me. At least then, her disconnect and the strange void around her aura would have made sense. My confusion would have had a piece of solid ground to fall down on.

Instead, I was left in utter confusion about who was looking after me. It felt like no one was. I felt out of place, often wondering if I was adopted—maybe that would explain my sense of isolation in the human world. And yet, I felt taken care of on the trail with Sumi. I felt love. I laughed, sang, and was able to be myself without apology or shame.

I have to remind myself that my mom was also a well-known physical therapist who healed so many people with state-of-the-art therapies. Her accolades were never mentioned at the dinner table. But I saw her gift of healing. Not only with animals but with humans too. She used to take me with her to the physical therapy clinic in Chinatown, where she worked with the elders. She lit up in a way I never saw at home. I watched my mom with fascination as she cared for her patients so gently and sweetly. Who was this other person? I only have a few fleeting memories of that kind of love from her when I was sick or injured.

Instead, we thought of her as a hypochondriac in our home because she would complain about this ailment or that. She was so self-absorbed in her own pain she couldn't really take care of us. I rarely saw her smile or laugh. When I look back at the photos of her as a young mom, I don't remember that lighter, more present woman. It was painful to see my mother so sad and depressed. I felt helpless to help her. As I grew into my womanhood, I watched her wither like a flower shriveling from lack of water. I tried to rescue her, but she lashed out in anger.

To most people, my mother was either sullen, void, or angry, but behind the veil, I saw an innocent wounded little girl. She was of the turtle clan, and like the turtle, she carried lifetimes of tragedy on her back. I felt compassion for her, but I would not allow myself to fall into her deep wallow. There had to be another way out.

I don't remember being hugged. I don't remember being loved and adored. And although Margaret wasn't touchy or emotionally soothing either, she did get out of bed every day. It was clear she was the matriarch of the family.

My mom was too sensitive to stand tall. She must have submitted too many times. I did not want to be like her. Not at all. But I had no other role models of a woman who stands tall. Margaret gave me a glimpse of what was possible, but her tactic was a bit hard-lined.

We used to call my dad the absent-minded professor because he was so deep in thought most of the time. He was often not home and left most of the parenting to my mother. He was excelling in his career and traveled around the world to give talks on PTSD and his research accomplishments. We were all proud of him. When he was home, he went into his study to work on his next book or paint until it was time for dinner. After dinner, he returned to his study. I preferred to go to his study with him and enjoy his quietness rather than watch TV with my brothers.

As I grew into a teenager, women like Gloria Steinem took on the media, shouting for women's rights. Our mothers had taught us how to be good wives, but Gloria and all the hippy women were shouting out for women's rights. What did that even mean?

They told us girls to think for ourselves. Yet, they had two sides. The "self-side" was passionate about their own interests, while the "wife-side" was all about their husbands. I was confused by the mixed messages: Be a good wife and mother, but no, be a career woman. It was challenging. Who was right? Who was wrong? Who do I listen to?

ROLE MODELS

- What was your relationship with your parents like?
- What was the energy like in your household?
- Were there other places where a different way of being was modeled that you admired?
- Who were your role models? They can be your parents or someone else in your life who had an influence on you.

I'll share one of my role models with you to spark some thought. After years and years of digging through the sandy terrain of my youth, looking for treasures and tidbits about who influenced me to be who I am today, I found a few role models who made a difference in my life. One such person was my sixth-grade teacher, Mrs. Burleson. She must have watched me draw on my desk, day in and day out, during English class. I hated school, and I didn't like English because I didn't think I was any good at it. One day, Mrs. Burleson came up to my desk and said, "Emma, I have a different assignment for you today. I'd like you to draw me ten pictures. Here's a book if you want to use it as a reference." And she handed me a book of animal illustrations.

I was beyond excited, "Really?"

"Yes," she said with a big warm smile.

I went home and happily drew all ten illustrations that same night and turned them in the next day, and I got all As. Thinking back on that offer makes so much sense. I think she literally kept me engaged in school. She saw my talent and passion for art, and she connected me there instead of forcing me into a place where I wilted. I am an artist to this day and am thankful she saw and supported me.

TIME IN NATURE CONTEMPLATION

Take a walk. If you can, find a quiet trail or a walking beach. As you walk, don't look down at the ground, but rather stand tall and let your feet know the path before you. Let your eyes look forward and peripherally to the side. Notice shapes, colors, movement. Breathe in and breathe out in a slow, steady way as you let your feet keep pace—feet, breath, earth, sky.

Say your name out loud to the plants and energies around you. Share out loud what you love. I am … I love … I am good at …

Allow a lightness of being to come into you.

Away from Home

Emma couldn't wait to leave home. When it came time to choose a college, her father insisted on UC Berkeley or UCLA because of their prestige. She tried to imagine herself living in the city. She was scared of the city. Cement was everywhere, and there were so few trees. Homeless people sat on dirty street corners begging for food. She wanted to take care of them, but she knew she couldn't. Her heart ached for them. Plus, the city was dangerous.

Emma knew her spirit would die in the city. She took her college planning into her own hands and found that UC Davis had lots of nature throughout the campus. It was known for its agriculture and veterinarian school. It also had a great art department and business school. She begged to go to UC Davis, using the excuse that her mother had gone there and her great-uncles too.

Her parents weren't thrilled with the idea. She knew one way that might change their mind. Her father had raised her to be a doctor. That was the way it was going to be. Even her grandfather, Morris, would say, "So, you're going to be a doctor when you grow up."

One night over dinner, Emma offered her choice of college. "I'd really like to go to UC Davis. It is a well-known college in the sciences. I could do all of the pre-med classes there."

They finally agreed. Emma made plans to bring Sumi with her, but her parents gave her a firm "no."

"No, Emma, you'll be distracted." A simple, one-liner: No.

Since Emma didn't pay the board bill, she didn't have much choice.

Her parents and brothers dropped her off at her new home, an old dormitory that her mother had also lived in in the early 1950s. Her new roommate seemed nice enough, a city girl, an only child, and quiet. The room, the size of a horse stall, was at the west end of a long narrow hallway, with numerous rooms off the north and east sides. The bathroom was all the way at the other end of the dorm, which meant day or night, Emma had to walk the long narrow corridor to do her bathroom business.

Emma felt strange for the first few weeks. So many new people, new smells, and no Sumi. Missing her horse, she rode her bike to the outskirts of town, looking for other horses. Dorm life was daunting, and there was no privacy, no secret world to escape to. She became very depressed. She was bored, out of her element, and surrounded by so many confusing people. She couldn't find quiet anywhere.

Emma remembered the blank sketchbook and nice black pen her aunt had given her for high school graduation. In her dark dorm room, she took it out and began drawing dragons. Happy dragons. She had never drawn dragons before. She wondered, *Why now?* In the past, all her drawings had to look realistic. Her whole life was supposed to look realistic. Now, her sketchbook became populated by a new fantasy world complete with mushrooms and trees—all of whom had faces and told whimsical stories.

Ariana Horowitz 1982

Drawing wasn't enough to connect her to the outdoors, so one day, she took her bike and rode out of town. Lo and behold, she found a horse stable where she began riding again. It became her routine to bike out to the Paso Fino barn twice a week between studies and tend to a dozen horses while their owners spent their time indoors getting drunk.

In addition to time with horses, she found an internship at the UC Davis Raptor Center, where she met Terry Schulz, who became a major influence on her. Terry was a man who felt all there was to feel and wore his heart on his sleeve. He was a man who carved owls in his sleep and taught youngsters how to listen to the birds. His love of nature was contagious.

Terry taught Emma about leadership and managing other students in the daily care of healing wounded or orphaned raptors. He was honest, reliable, and sincere. He rewarded her for jobs well done. It was the first time Emma ever felt praise, and she loved it. Her commitment to the Raptor Center was apparent, and she soon became a team leader and trained other students how to handle the birds.

Emma felt at home at the Raptor Center. The hawks, eagles, and owls were wise and reminded her of her own visceral knowledge of animal communication. She found an acceptance in the quiet solitude of their presence as they allowed her to heal them, a gift they gave each day. They were wise and intelligent beings. They could see into her thoughts and through her imagination. She was awestruck by how well they saw through her vulnerability. Like the horses, they knew the truth within her heart and would only meet her there.

As she deepened her studies in pre-veterinary medicine, she took up several shifts at the UC Davis School of Veterinary Medicine, including the non-domestics ward. Injured raptors and other wild animals began their healing journey amid the barren steel cages and grey floors.

Emma loved caring for the wounded animals. Her most exciting afternoons in the non-domestic ward were spent holding raptors, alligators, snakes, lions, turtles, exotic birds, and opossums while the veterinarian worked on their injuries. She felt like she had met them all before, like they were old friends. She gently looked into their eyes as they looked back at her.

"You'll be okay; we are here to help you with your wounds," she whispered with native wisdom. "If you stay still, we will be done quickly. Stay with me. I will keep you safe."

An exchange followed between Emma and the animals, each connecting in an ancient knowing, each healing the other. Emma wasn't aware of it then, but the animals gave her a solid ground to be herself in the midst of all the people around her. Even the veterinarians, with their quirky social nuances, were like her in a quiet way.

Emma had found her place away from home. She spent more time between the Raptor Center, the non-domestic ward, and the horse ranches where she worked than she spent in the classroom. These places were second best to the ocean, now several hours away.

Once a month, she took the Greyhound bus home to spend the weekend with Sumi. Riding on the beach was the breath of fresh air she needed to keep going at the drier interior landscape of college.

Each time she came home, her parents would ask her how her pre-med studies were going.

"Fine," is all she had to say.

Back at school, she had gained enough veterinary experience to get paid jobs in the small animal ward. She took home a couple of puppies and some cats she rescued, even though her parents told her not to. At one point, she had three jobs at the vet school: one before dawn, another at noon, and a third at the end of the day.

Every day was a different day with different dilemmas related to the animals. The veterinarians gave her a lot of responsibility, which she thrived on and met fully. They, too, acknowledged her for her skill with animals. She felt seen in a way she had not felt seen before. Even though the veterinarians were people of few words, they acknowledged her skill with animals and gave her more responsibility than the other employees. To Emma, that was a reward. It meant she had value.

On the academic side, her studies in animal behavior conflicted with her hands-on experiences with animals. The animal behavior professor, the authority figure who handed out pass or fail grades, insisted to Emma and the other young students that animals have no thoughts or feelings.

"Animals don't have emotions," he pontificated as if humans were somehow of a higher order, separate from the animal world.

Emma was appropriately disturbed. "That can't be so, Professor," she said, with a hint of rebellion in her voice.

The professor glared at her through his rimmed glasses, his beard tightening in invisible knots of irritation. "Emma, this is so," he instructed. "For example, baby wolves don't play. They mimic the actions they will need to take when they are adults. Actions like fighting and killing prey."

"What about otters?" she asked. "Aren't they clearly expressing joy when they are playing?"

"No, Emma, they do not feel joy, nor are they playing. The monkeys in the research lab are not sad."

"But we humans feel emotions when we see otters playing or see a monkey in a cage which looks sad. We feel their emotions. We resonate with them," she tried again.

"No, Emma, the science of biology is a system of rules, and there is no scientific evidence that animals have emotions. And they certainly don't have feelings like we do. Now let's move on," he said dismissively.

Emma sat down with tears in her eyes. Once again, she witnessed the reckless stupidity of man. Once again, man had spoken. He had declared a reality she did not believe in: "We must dominate the natural world. Since animals don't feel or have emotions, we can experiment on them. Give them cancers and HIV so we can find cures for people," the scientists declared. Emma was disgusted.

She felt powerless to defend the brilliance of the magical interconnectedness she knew in her heart. How could people be so arrogant to think that somehow we are separate from the earth and all her creations? It made no sense. No sense at all.

She read in textbooks how industrial human societies made up philosophical rationalizations about the meaning of life to support whatever they wanted to dominate: plants, animals, and even people. The tension between the pretense and lies of the human world and the honesty of nature grew stronger.

Emma wondered if others could feel the disconnectedness of humans and the corresponding betrayal of the earth by the two-legged ones who dominated with the power of an almighty god to control and manipulate anything or anyone who was inconvenient. Could she learn to step away from the resulting despair and anger and walk in the human world? She couldn't turn her back on her animal friends. They were authentic and always connected to a higher source. They saw into her very being and welcomed her into their world.

As the stark difference between nature's realness and the human world's distorted sense of what was true grew into a rushing river with two very different shores, Emma knew her place on the wild side. As she slowly became more and more disconnected from people, she disappeared further into her private world with animals and nature.

She tried to find solace with her boyfriend, who visited a few times a month. But she still felt alone when she was not with the animals. On one occasion, her boyfriend convinced her to have sex when she wasn't feeling well, and the condom he used broke. Two weeks later, she knew she was pregnant. She went home ashamed, afraid to tell her parents, but knew she had to.

Once home and her secret revealed, Emma's parents whisked her off to get an abortion without even having a conversation about her choices. Her mother, father, and brothers waited outside while the nurses took her into a narrow room. There was a large vacuum sound, and she felt great pain. She started to cry. It was the cry of a young mother losing her baby. Her cry was so deep even the forest at the foothills of her childhood wept.

Once home, she crawled into bed, covered her head, and wept some more. Emotions of loss overwhelmed her, and she was ill-equipped to deal with the pain inside. Her mother brought her a cup of tea and closed the door.

"Emma, never tell anyone you came home to get an abortion. Don't even tell your roommate you got pregnant. People look down on girls who have sex before marriage and, worse yet, girls who get pregnant outside of wedlock. Remember your friend Alexa who got pregnant in high school? She lost all of her friends, and she had to quit school. How could you let this happen to you" Her mother's shameful words found a dark place in Emma's wounded heart.

Emma fell into a great depression when she returned to school. Her roommate knew something was wrong, but Emma tried to keep her secret, making an already awkward socializing experience worse. Now there was tension with her roommate and everyone on the dorm floor.

When Emma had to walk down the narrow hall to use the restroom, she bowed her head in shame and looked at the dirty carpet on the floor as she passed the other students who had been her friends.

One day, a cashier shortchanged her five dollars. She knew it, but she had no courage to call him on it and ask for her change. She went home and wept. She had never lost herself like this before.

A year after the abortion, Emma knew something was very wrong, and she knew she had to go home to get help. Emma took a Greyhound bus to San Francisco, where her mother picked her up. They drove in silence all the way home. After dinner, Emma tried to help her mom by doing the dishes. Her mom broke the silence. "What is going on with you, Emma?"

Emma started to cry. "I don't know what is wrong with me. I'm so sad. I cry all the time. I can't look people in the eye. I think I need to see a therapist. I never got over the abortion. I want my baby back, and I know that is not going to solve my pain."

Her mother turned into Jekyll and Hyde. "How dare you try to one-up me!"

"Mom, I have no idea what you are talking about," Emma said as tears streamed down her face.

"You got pregnant, so you could prove you could have children, and I cannot."

Emma fell to the floor in a puddle of tears. Her head swirled in every direction, looking for which way was up. She looked up into her mother's eyes and pleaded, "Mom, you can't say that."

"It's true!" Her mother's face was distorted in a quiet but fierce rage. "You got pregnant right after I had a hysterectomy. Just to rub it in my face!"

Emma couldn't believe what was happening. She had come home to ask for help, to get some love. She longed for someone to hold her tight and tell her everything was going to be okay—that she was okay. She felt as if her mother had given her a death sentence.

"I didn't know you had a hysterectomy. I would never try to hurt you."

Her mother stood towering over her limp body for what seemed like an eternity. How could her mother be so cruel? Emma knew in her heart that if her mother did not take back her shameful words, she would never be able to speak to her again. Somehow she found the strength to pick herself up off the floor. With her feet planted solidly on the floor, she took a deep breath and looked her mother straight on. "Mother," she said quietly, but with great purpose, "you need to take those words away, or I will never be able to speak to you again."

She didn't wait for her mother's reply. She disappeared out the door and followed the bramble bush trail to the creek behind her house. This place had always been her secret hideaway spot in case she was ever hunted. She went deeper into her own interior, where the animals were her guides and the trees were her parents. The waters along the creek were her intuitive medium, the place that had no words. She found herself gasping for air in the shallow waters. She felt like she had been shot in the heart, like a wounded deer hidden in the forest.

The Death of Love

I saw it happen.
The death of love that day.
The kind of love that flows from an open heart
That gives without a need in return.
The kind of love that breathes fresh air into tired lungs
And awakens the spirit's journey back to life,
Channeling tears of sadness into streams of hope.

This love overflowed from the red mare's heart
To all the strangers that visited her home.
She filled the barn with possibility and light.

But alas,
Her innocence ignored by the human's pride,
Assuming her love would flow forever,
And that her heart would never close.

They wanted her to dance for them all day and night
As they amused themselves with their self-grandeur,
Allowing their selfishness to dominate their way,

They filled their chests with her open heart
Hoping their troubles would fall away.

And then one day it happened.
Her innocence betrayed
In the flash of an eye, her wisdom shunted.
What happened dare you say,
That things could turn out this way?

Well, the invisible monster of self-absorption
So consumed the stranger who had come to get love
He forgot why he had come.

This man, his heart filled with lack,
Took a whip to this red mare,
And before anyone could stop him
He punished her open heart,
With the sting of his whip upon her flesh.

The red mare was so surprised!
She turned and looked at the stranger with wild eyes.
Her heart abused; her innocence lost.
Fear had won; love had lost.
I saw it happen.

Opportunities and Contemplations

REFLECTION

After the abortion, I truly became separated from the human world. I lost all confidence. I didn't recognize myself. I was really on my own, and I didn't know what to do. The abortion had set a symphony of instincts rushing through me to get my baby back. All I could think about was being a mom, wanting to be a mom. I had to remind myself that that was unrealistic. I sought out a therapist and slowly started to put myself back together.

To this day, I can't fathom how my mom could have been so cruel at such a crucial time in my life. I had no friends to talk to. In some way, it reaffirmed that there must be something wrong with me for not seeing what she touted as the obvious.

Interesting that this inner deterioration to my self-esteem coincided with the lies my animal behavior professors were telling me. It's like the authority figures in my life, my mother and my professors—those people we are supposed to listen to and believe—were hell-bent on proving they had dominion over animals. This way, they could be "superior" and have governing say about what animals (myself included) could or could not feel.

At the time, I was too naïve to realize I was disgusted and felt deeply disrespected. The only thing I knew to do was acquiesce and hope for their approval. It was easier for me to defend animals than to defend myself. I couldn't believe the professors taught such narrow and untrue views of nature and animals. I was treated like "a girl" who didn't know better. But inside, I knew they were wrong.

It wasn't until 2019, when I heard Jane Goodall share in a documentary a similar experience of being looked down on as a woman, that I started to look back at this period of my life to reflect on how it shaped me as a self, as a woman, and as a human.

Through reflection and writing, I began to see this much deeper programming about who I was supposed to be. I was supposed to be pretty, graceful, a good wife, and a good hostess. I was supposed to be an intellectual. Animals, dirt, and the natural world were not part of this program. And being a free spirit was definitely not part of this program.

The people who were supposed to guide and teach me said animals don't have emotions; they don't feel. How dare I even breathe a word that I know animals not only feel but speak! Was my whole being wrong?

It was clear that if I didn't follow the logic of the professors, my mother, and my family—*if I didn't become who they wanted me to be*—then I would fail at the one thing I yearned for: my mother and father's love. I felt like I had failed to get an ounce of the approval I so deeply longed for from my family.

Somewhere in this struggle, I chose animals over people.

NOT SEEN

Reflect on a time when you felt like your experience, your values, and what you believed clashed with an authority figure in your life. It could be a parent, an elder, or a member of your community.

- What conclusion did you come to?
- What story did you tell yourself?
- How did you feel?
- How did you reconcile that difference between your view and theirs? Or did you?

TIME IN NATURE CONTEMPLATION

Find a quiet place where you can get close to the earth. Feel the protection of the elements around you. Feel the solidness of the trees or the rocks, the firmness of the soil. Thank each of them for seeing you.

Notice if any animals or birds are with you in this quiet place. Allow nature, the animals, and birds to have emotions, to share their mood with you.

Notice the quality of energy around you. Notice how your energy changes as you spend time in nature. Does the old story, the limiting view, stay with you here? Or does it disappear?

Wounded Raptors

Emma couldn't wait to get back to the Raptor Center, her quiet place of solace. Usually, there were no people there, only the birds. There was one bird that had become Emma's best friend. He was a beautiful red-tailed hawk, and his name was RT17. He sat at the back of his pen, in the shadows, trying to stay hidden from sight. Emma thought he looked like she had just days before: her little wounded deer self hidden in the forest. The hawk's head was turned down in grief, and his feathers tucked up tight against his body.

As Emma approached RT17, she pretended she was not in pain. She tried to put her pain aside because she had work to do. Besides, RT17 had more to be sad about. He had lost his wing. A raptor without a wing dies quickly in the wild. Someone found him in a field, dragging his wing and unable to fly. The bones in his wing were shattered from a BB gun, and his wing had to be amputated. The veterinarian chose to keep the hawk alive rather than euthanize him because there was something special about "his way of being" that would make a good teaching bird.

He became one of the "non-releaseables," a band of birds that would never see freedom again but whose story could inspire humans to respect these beautiful birds of prey. Terry, her bird teacher, taught Emma how to teach a raptor to stand on her fist like they do in falconry. The art of falconry goes back over four thousand years, and many cultures tell stories of the special bond between man and bird, a special relationship of trust and mutual respect.

"Do you want to know why it was so important to get these majestic birds into visibility as our brothers and sisters?" he asked. "One of the main reasons we train these birds to stand on our hand is so we can teach young people about why the birds are so important for our ecosystem. In this way, people will learn not to kill them. Too many farmers and ranchers think these birds kill their chickens, so they teach their children to shoot them dead. We can change that, Emma."

"I'm all for that. I wish we could save all one-winged raptors to be our falconry partners so that we can heal each other. Why can't we save all of them?"

"Maybe someday we can do that too, Emma." Terry agreed.

However, RT17 was becoming a lost cause. No one wanted to work with him. He was too depressed. He wouldn't even try to stand on anyone's fist. Even the best falconers at the Raptor Center had given up on him.

Today, Emma felt a new sense of intention to get RT17 over his self-defeat. She would not, could not, give up on him. If he failed to succumb to standing on a man's (or woman's) hand in captivity, he would be euthanatized. She would have none of that. He had too many gifts left to give.

"If you do not learn to come out and socialize a bit, the humans will give up on you," she said.

"I don't care," he said with his head bent down. The one wing he had left lay slumped and lifeless.

"Well, I do!" Emma said. "You are so beautiful. If you learn to stand on my fist, you will have the important task of teaching children how majestic and wise you are. You will go to schools and stand proudly on the human's fist while they teach young people not to shoot birds like you."

"Why would I want to face the little bastards who shot me?" he said bitterly. "That makes no sense at all. They can go to hell!"

Emma's tears fell on the dry, dusty, lifeless dirt at her feet. "I understand completely," she said. "I know it doesn't make sense, but we can only hope they didn't know better. Maybe no one taught them to be respectful. The boy who shot you told the hospital he thought you were bad. He thought you ate his parents' chickens."

"That is absurd. Why do people tell such lies? I've never eaten a chicken, and I never will."

"I know you are innocent, and what has happened to you is wrong. And I know our only hope is that you can teach humans another way of being. If you show them your beautiful feathers and allow your piercing eyes to look into their souls the way you look into mine, they will see you for who you are. They will see their reflection in the mirror of you. They will see your wild brothers and sisters with new eyes. They will be changed. And maybe together, you and I can change the world one small person at a time."

Emma tried to place RT17 on her fist. He kept his talons clenched, his eyes squinted, and he looked at her through a sliver of light. He half-opened his talons in a half-hearted attempt and fell dangling by his leather ties under her leather-gloved hand. She scooped him up again and put him against her chest so he could feel her heartbeat.

"Please, RT17, please do this for me." She put her hand out again and held him over it. This time, he put his clenched talons on her glove.

"Open your talons and stand on my hand. I promise I will hold you up."

RT17 looked deeply into her soul and saw her smiling heart. Then he opened his left talon wide and grabbed her leather glove.

"It's okay," Emma said. "You won't hurt me with your sharp talons because the gloves are so thick. Go ahead and grab on—just like that."

RT17 opened his right talon.

"Yes, yes, just like that! Now I am going to take my hand off your back so you can stand up by yourself."

Emma gently removed her hand, and RT17 gave her his full weight.

"I'm doing it. I'm doing it, Emma!" he said.

"Yay, this is the best day ever!" Emma cheered.

The two went off on their first walk together, side by side. The hot sun pressed on their backs as they strode through the meadows where RT17 used to fly free. They watched the grasshoppers bounce and pop. When a mouse scurried by, RT17 thought for a moment about following it, but he knew he could not fly with only one wing. And so, he trusted Emma to be his wings as they walked to the creek to catch the fragrant water glimmering in its freedom flow.

Emma and RT17 spent many years together after that. RT17 went on to become one of the most important and respected raptors of the youth education program.

She didn't realize it at the time, but RT17 reflected Emma's own heart. He had given up, and so had she. She had asked him to come back into the world, and he had shown her how to do it. He trusted her and believed her story that he could help make the world a better place. He gave her his full weight; he opened his talons and stood tall without apology.

Emma never forgot RT17. She often sent him messages on the intuitive internet of time and space. His beautiful presence was etched in her memory forever.

She learned something important from RT17 and the other animals and horses in her care. While some of them could rip her flesh or even kill her if they wanted to, they didn't. They trusted her. They sensed that she was there to offer them assistance, to help them heal. They relaxed their bodies into her hands, looked into her eyes, and silent conversations ensued. Each shared stories with the other. They connected through invisible threads that wove them to the underworld. There was no urgency in this timeless place.

It didn't seem to make a difference if it was a great horned owl, a bald eagle, an alligator, or a black panther. The language of animals was universal. Why, then, was it so hard for humans to listen and speak to animals? How wide was the river between them? Why couldn't humans remember this intuitive place of connection?

Emma thought about the work RT17 was doing to change the world. What was her calling? Was it really a bridge she was to build? Or was she going to have to teach every human how to swim in the watery unknown?

The Call of the Wild

You raised me too close to the forest and the open spaces
Where deer and rabbits run their races.

I caught a glimpse of the hawk's glance
And the way the water skeeters prance
The appeal of the wild too strong to resist
My free spirit does persist

My boots chalked with mud
My dusty jacket like a wet rug
I jump on my mare and head for the hills
The appeal too strong to live within the frills

Wild and free I am
Wild and free I am
As I run with the deer
The hawk flies near

Together finding balance in the thicket and grass
Sending prayers of freedom to those that trespass

May those whose hearts closed long ago
Let their imagination out to play
And in this wildness, find a new way.

Opportunities and Contemplations

REFLECTION

Even though I was far away from the sea and my favorite creeks while I attended UC Davis, the raptors gave me a quiet place to be me. Oddly enough, the road to the center was along Putah Creek (which means where the whores go to wash their clothes), a waterway that snaked its way slowly but steadily to the San Francisco Bay.

I was extremely proud of rescuing RT17 and happily educating children and adults on how amazing raptors are and how necessary they are to our habitats. He's a major reason why I specialized in birds of prey. I had an identity at the Raptor Center. I was leading and teaching younger college students how to work with the birds and be quiet with their energy so the birds would allow them to approach.

RT17 and the lessons he taught me came back to me when my personal life was unraveling. I felt like I had lost my courage to stand tall like I had asked him to do. Even the metaphor of his missing wing rang true for me.

I heard that he had succumbed to a viral disease that had swept through the Raptor Center and had passed away. I felt like a part of me wanted to die with him. But I immediately remembered how brave he was, and his memory reminded me that I needed to be brave in this time of sorrow.

He reminded me that I did not give up on him, even though everyone else had. It felt like everyone was giving up on me. He reminded me not to give up. He had my back, our roles had reversed, and he was now asking me to take a stand for myself. Had I become "non-releasable"? Was I no longer able to be free, to fly with my own two wings?

By talking with him in the spirit world and journaling about our time together, I uncovered a very important piece of my subconscious. It was a piece I desperately needed, as my essence was being consumed by the extreme disconnect I felt between the human world and the animal world.

I continue to be amazed by how the right guide comes in when I need it the most. RT17 reminded me to have courage and not give up. And, more importantly, that we are never truly alone. Nature is always right outside our door.

AWAY FROM HOME

- Do you remember a time when you were out of your element or felt lost or disconnected from others?
- Or a time when you gave up on yourself?
- What did it feel like?
- How did you make sense of it?
- Like RT17 and Emma became friends, who were your friends or resources during that time?
- How did you take care of yourself? Or not?
- Where did you find courage in adversity?
- Can you summon it when you need it?
- How do you reconnect to yourself, your true essence?

TIME IN NATURE CONTEMPLATION

Take a walk outside and notice how many birds you see. Ask them what they see. Who are they? How do they relate to each other? What is the quality or tone of their voice? What is the mood with which they are conversing?

Does it feel like the birds are noticing you?

Is there a bird or animal that comes to you more often than others, especially when you are out of sorts with yourself?

Motherhood

Emma took on more responsibility at the Raptor Center. She was in charge of the birds that could potentially heal enough to be released back into the wild. The birds came to the center after they recovered from their original injury, usually a damaged wing or sometimes a leg injury. The rehab process included massaging the muscles of the injured wing, hoping to bring it back to a complete range of motion. Emma knew there was a better way, having grown up watching her mom do all kinds of crazy healing methods.

She brought her mom out to help her develop a physical therapy program for the injured birds that included more than massaging the atrophied muscles. Together they created charts to track daily progress and specific exercises for each potentially releasable bird. They created a physical therapy protocol that had never existed for raptors in rehabilitation before.

Emma handled the birds and knew how they flew. She understood their wing function and the aerodynamics of flight. Her mom knew about range of motion and exercises to loosen and strengthen atrophied muscles. At that time, birds with a wing injury were wrapped up at the vet school to prevent the injured wing from moving. The problem was the wing became frozen within three weeks, due to lack of motion.

"Okay, Emma, you know how the bird flies. I want you to hold the bird at his legs; then I want you to raise and lower the bird to mimic his flight pattern. First, I have to measure the range of motion before we do anything," her mom instructed.

Emma watched with fascination the special tools her mom used to measure the range of motion in each of the joints of the bird's wing. She measured the good wing and the injured wing for comparison and kept meticulous notes.

"Okay, hold the bird to your chest with the bird facing outward. Now lift him over your head. Since this bird's injured wing is the left one, I want you to drop him to the left. Drop his body down and to the left swiftly, so he has to try to catch himself with his bad wing. You see, in this way, we will help him regain strength by using his reflexive muscles. His reflexive muscles and instincts are good, and hopefully, he will slowly regain flexibility and strength in the atrophied muscles. This will improve his range of motion and rebuild his muscle memory post-trauma."

Emma did as her mother said. She could feel the bird trying to stretch his frozen muscles. She would silently tell the bird, "You can do it! We're going to kick this injury." The mother, daughter, and bird repeated this several times per session. At the end of the session, they measured the range of motion, and lo and behold, it had improved.

Over the next several months, Emma and her mom were able to increase the releasability of wounded raptors at the center by over 45 percent. Emma wrote a paper about it to present at a conference back East. She and her mom were going to present their results together. This could be Emma's way into the job market, doing what she loved: working with raptors.

Emma remembered going to conferences as a child and watching her father give presentations. She loved conferences—so many ideas presented and information to be inspired by. This was her turn to be a part of a conference. She was excited to meet other raptor specialists and share what she and her mom had learned. At the conference, however, her mother took over the lecture. She didn't acknowledge Emma and didn't admit it was Emma's idea in the first place. Her mother didn't see this as an opportunity for Emma to show her innovative idea, her success, and to potentially make a career for herself. Instead, she stole Emma's light, and Emma came home disempowered and forlorn.

Emma couldn't wait to graduate and do something else. After five long years at UC Davis, Emma graduated with a bachelor's degree in zoology with a specialty in animal behavior and a minor in art. She returned to the coastal towns of her childhood. Sumi was still boarded at Muir Beach Stables. Emma didn't waste a moment in returning to her daily ritual of riding the beaches and wildlands around the ocean's edge.

Her first summer at home, Emma's parents had moved out of their Mill Valley house to be on sabbatical at Stanford. There wasn't room for Emma at their temporary home, so she lived out of her mother's Toyota Chinook with two rescue dogs and two cats. She worked several jobs. She cared for horses at Muir Beach, healed wounded animals at the local veterinary hospital, and waitressed at night. She still lived between the two worlds—keeping busy in the animal world by day and the human world at night.

Emma's life had a routine schedule. But a little surprise came unexpectedly. Emma was pregnant again. Emma knew she would have this baby no matter what. She was not going to give her up, *not for nothing and not for nobody.*

In her third month of pregnancy, she married the father on New Year's Eve. It seemed like the right thing to do.

Her parents were still expecting her to "be somebody." She had decided not to pursue medical school, and she had learned from working at the vet school (morning, noon, and night) that a vet had no life. How would she be able to have a family and be a veterinarian? She couldn't see it. So, she decided not to be a veterinarian either.

Now pregnant, she had no idea where she was headed. Her potential raptor career in raptor rehab was gone. She had a few offers in distant states to do owl studies, but being pregnant made those jobs virtually impossible. She was demoralized about her career or lack thereof. She still worked with animals every day. But she could see no career ladder in her future as a vet tech or even a horse trainer.

One day, twenty-four weeks into her pregnancy, she didn't feel well. She asked her boss at the Sausalito Animal Clinic if she could go home for the rest of the afternoon. By then, her parents had gotten a divorce, and her mother lived in a little houseboat in Sausalito. She went to her mom's while waiting for her husband to be off work.

"Emma, lie down and let me feel your belly," her mother insisted.

After a few minutes, her mother said, concerned, "Emma, you are in premature labor. You are having contractions. You need to go to the hospital now." Her mother had been one of the first Lamaze childbirth coaches and knew all about pregnancy and early baby development. She took Emma to the hospital.

After a three-day stay in the hospital to stop the labor, Emma had to lie in bed for the next ten weeks. Emma didn't take the premature labor seriously until the nurses took her to the preemie ward. "Your baby will live here if she survives."

"Well, then I will stay here with her," Emma said confidently.

"No. No, you won't. You will have to go home every day and leave her here."

That was not at all acceptable to Emma. She knew they were serious, and she had to lie down.

Even though Emma was known as the Energizer Bunny, she handled the confinement well. Her baby's daddy surrounded her bed with knitting, sketching, and reading projects to keep her busy while he went to work trimming trees. They were so poor they didn't even have a refrigerator, so he went to the store every evening for food supplies and happily made dinner.

Mae was born three weeks early and was the most amazing jewel Emma had ever seen. Five pounds six ounces and born with the cutest little smile on her face. Emma spent days looking into Mae's sparkling eyes. Mae smiled back at her gleefully, filling Emma's heart with unimaginable love. This baby changed everything. Emma knew the minute she held Mae to her chest that she had to learn how to embrace her feminine powers, the powers she had denied all these years, to care for her babe.

Motherhood was like coming home to herself—a time in which all her ancient knowing appeared and guided her. Keoki, her ancestral grandmother, visited her in spirit when she was nursing, and together they sang lullabies passed down on silent waves.

Emma's mom was smitten with Mae. She came alive in a way that Emma had never seen before. For a brief time, a bond formed between them that Emma had longed for her whole life. Her mother shared stories of her parents and her grandparents. Emma's mother's mother had passed away when Emma was only five, so only a hint of her essence was left in Emma's memory.

Ancestors on her mother's side were from native families in Ireland and the Welsh territories and had come over on the Mayflower in the late 1600s. They became founders of Huntington, West Virginia. Stories of her great-grandmothers were few and far between. The only female ever talked about was Keoki. She was Emma's great-grandmother of Seneca descent. She was a native child. Her name sat awkwardly on the family tree, to the side of everyone else.

The story has it she was adopted into the family as a child. When she was in her early teens, one of the men in the family had his way with her, and nine months later she gave birth to a little girl, Emma's Grandmother

Lucy. The baby was taken from her, and she was sent off to a nunnery. No one ever talked about why Emma's Grandmother Lucy had such long black hair, while her sister and cousins were more fair-skinned and on the blonder side. Emma shared Keoki's darker skin, native ways, and high cheekbones.

Keoki went unacknowledged; her tribal heritage was never spoken about. Yet, Emma's mom often talked about Keoki and how she had been sent off to a nunnery, even though the family was not religious. Emma always felt baffled. Keoki seemed important, so why was she not honored in the family tree? Did Emma get her natural ways from Keoki?

When Mae was born, Emma's mom sang Keoki's lullaby to her, just as she had sung it to Emma when she was a little girl.

One day when Emma's mom was holding Mae, a big smile on her face, she softly spoke, "I always wanted your middle name to be Keoki."

"Why didn't you do that?" Emma queried.

"Your dad didn't like the idea, so I got talked into having your middle name be Karen, like your aunt."

"Why didn't you stand up for what you wanted, Mom? Keoki means so much more to me. I don't identify with Karen at all; it doesn't seem like my real middle name." Now Emma felt like a tiny sliver of her ancestry, her link to Keoki, was real. She felt it in her bones. Yet no one had taken a stand for that part of her lineage.

In her heart, Emma knew that she and Keoki shared a timeless bond. She felt her looking over Emma in her invisible, ancient, knowing way. Emma missed her terribly. Emma had always felt torn away from her original family, a feeling of loss so deep it could not be healed. But she had had no reason to know why she felt that way. Anytime she asked about ancestors, she had been shut down.

For as long as she could remember, Emma had felt like the rug was going to be pulled out from under her. She had a strange fear that the land was going to be seized from her embrace. Emma could never understand this odd fear she felt. The glimpse of Keoki in her past gave her a cookie crumb and an intuitive trail of memory. But because, even now, no one acknowledged it, she again felt alone in her ancient knowing.

Holding her daughter, Mae, in her arms made Emma yearn to know more about her ancestors. Her mother often told of Emma's other great-grandmother on her father's side, who was part Cherokee and Irish. But again, the family would not recognize any native heritage, just as the native heritage on her mother's side was never discussed. It was like her mother's ancestry, the Irish-Welsh-Native blend had no place. And so, a significant part of Emma's imagination was left to blood memory.

Emma knew how to plant corn, beans, and squash, although no one had taught her. She knew how to bead without knowing how she knew. As a girl, she didn't think much of it, but she had an ancient way with the earth that had been passed down on silent trails of wisdom woven into the depths of her knowing. These were trails she followed but did not know why.

Without realizing it, Emma felt connected to her great-grandmothers through art, beadwork, and even in her hands as she tended the soil. One day, she remembered she had always been connected to her great-grand-mothers, at least, in the spirit world. They had not left her, even though they were not acknowledged. She felt her great-grandmothers teaching her things through her newfound motherhood. They taught her about the soil, and they agreed that the dragonfly carried goodwill and the raven was always to be one of her guides.

Emma went outside to smell the garden roses one chilly morning while Mae slept. A dragonfly rested on a flush pink rose. Her bright red wings were an intricate web of interconnection and so shiny like they had been sprayed with some kind of glittery glaze.

"Isn't that wondrous?" Keoki's voice floated in the wind.

"You can see it too?" Emma asked.

"Oh, yes, and you can see too, dear one."

"Why does it feel so hard? If I tell someone what I see, they look at me oddly or like I am too out there. I'm scared to share with others what I see. It makes sense to me, but I feel very alone with what I see."

"There will come a day, Emma, when you won't feel so alone. Someday you will have to share what you see to help save our forests, native animals, and plants. Someday, you will have to raise your voice loud and clear. The ravens already know they must be your guardians. They will give you affirmations and warnings. They have your back." And with that, Keoki's spirit disappeared into the raspberry patch and beyond.

"Great. I have no idea what she just said. But I think she gave me a lot of responsibility," Emma muttered as she filled her hand with a few berries and chugged them down like candy.

"Yum, yum, thank you," she expressed, and then, off she went.

Emma wanted to know more about her father's ancestors, too, so she could teach Mae about her family of origin. She learned that her father's parents immigrated to the United States from Austria and Poland just before World War II. Her Grandfather Morris left the family's potato farm after he was a prisoner of war in World War I and fled to America as his family's land was being seized. He saved his money and brought over four of his five brothers and sisters before the Nazis officially began persecuting the Jews. His people were torn away from the farm and their homes. Only a picture of the old farmhouse remained—buried in a box for over fifty years.

Her father's mother, Lillian, came to America from Austria on a ship as a young teenager. Even though she was petite, she was quite savvy. She dressed classy, beyond her means. She was a seamstress for the wealthy in Los Angeles. She always held her head up high, as if she, too, was one of her wealthy clients. Lillian taught Emma how to sew and knit. Sitting next to her grandmother as Lillian gently guided Emma with her soft words, Emma felt her quiet strength. Lillian taught her how to make a mean chicken soup from chicken legs and scraps. She taught her how to make the best out of a little.

Lillian always had flowers planted outside her front door and houseplants purposely placed in the right spot to remind her of nature. When Lillian passed away at ninety-four, Emma kept three pairs of her gloves, each a different color, her hand-beaded sweater, and her favorite evening coat.

I Am She and She Is I

Why do I feel so deeply the earthly patterns?
The spiral in the eye of the hawk?

Why do I feel so far away from my people?
I want to go back.

I want my great-grandmother to know that I remember.
I yearn to live the way my blood runs, like a hot ember.

I see her face,
Tears kindly embrace.
My pain looks away, wanting to stray
To far off fields where lizards play.
But she calls me back.
She gives no slack.
More tears fall,
I must stand tall.

And yet, I am angry
I am afraid,
I begin to fray and walk away
The tears come faster now.
I can't stop them furrowing my brow.

My great-grandmother's glance
Has taken me in her trance
Her beadwork is gifted from my hand
It is in my blood, as is this land.
Passed down on a silent trail of tears,
Inviting all witnesses to shift gears
From greed and consumption
To compassion without presumption.

And so, I prevail, with only the memory of her
Feeding all who come a cookie and a prayer.
Her brightness shining down on me
Like a full moon overlooking the sea.

She gives me strength once again
To walk among those in pain
As it is my gift
However thrift.

I am she and she is I
And we will never die.

Opportunities and Contemplations

REFLECTION

Having my first child sent me into a deeper curiosity of my family background. I think becoming a parent naturally causes a person to reflect on his or her parents and perhaps even their grandparents.

I have profound connections to the blood memory of my forefathers. As I journaled and looked back for a cookie-crumb trail to the angst of my current situation, I began to see a thread of my inner subconscious deeply linked to my ancestors. For instance, even though I have done a lot of work on myself, I have a deep fear that my land will be taken away. This fear that the rug under my feet will be ripped away and my spirit will be taken is in the very foundation of my roots on both sides of my mother and my father's ancestors. No wonder I felt so amiss for so long! How often are we taking on the burdens, the traumas, of our ancestors?

From childhood into motherhood and progressing through adulthood, I always felt a loneliness, a feeling of being lost from my ancestors. A fear permeated under the surface of my being that I could never quite put my finger on. Even through years of therapy and self-development, I had no words to express how deep this fear was for me. By writing down on paper my interpretation of the stories of my family, I began to see an overwhelming pattern of loss—of place, dignity, home, and freedom.

I became fascinated with the idea of blood memory. I witnessed in my equine-guided work how some people were gripped by deep fears that paralyzed their progress. It was oftentimes unrelated to their present-life experience, making it difficult to find the source. Yet, the horses had a way of taking people to a place that was not in the present time. Sometimes an ancestor or loved one who had passed spoke to them through the horse as a channel.

At first, I thought to myself, *Well, it doesn't have to be true. I don't have to prove that this is possible, but what if some of my pain, fears, and feelings of deep loss are feelings passed down in my blood?*

As I opened more into this idea, it became a pathway for me to sort out what is mine and what has been passed down through my lineage. With that knowledge, I can now choose a new approach. I can acknowledge my ancestors. I can listen. And I can change the story that gets passed down to the next generation. I can break the link of pain.

I'm still unraveling the jewels of my ancestry, like little shards of crystals stuck in a spider web—so rich, so interconnected, and so potentially freeing.

HONORING OUR ANCESTORS AND ELDERS

All of our ancestors prior to the 1800s had some native roots and ancient traditions passed down for thousands of years. Whether they were from Europe, the Americas, Asia, Africa, or other parts of the world, all our early ancestors lived close to the earth.

- Which of your ancestors do you resonate with most? Even if you don't remember them, imagine them. Maybe you can even look up their culture and the land they came from.
- Is there a grandparent you looked up to? Can you bring the virtues of this person to the present? Maybe this person can be your guide now.
- What was the land like where your ancestors lived?
- If you choose, write a poem for this person.

TIME IN NATURE CONTEMPLATION

Go outside and find a tree, rock, meadow, or a waterway, and ask your ancestors to join you in contemplation.

Do you have any guidance you would like to ask for? Ask them what they see or if they can offer you any guidance. If they left you before you could say your peace, you could say it now. The place where you are, its animals and plants, whoever you are with, may be able to channel your thoughts on your behalf.

The World of People

Mae was a social delight. Communicating with people was easy for her. Emma admired her social ability and began to learn from Mae that people could be interesting animals also. Mae's natural presence with people forced Emma to be more social. All the people in town knew Mae by name; thus, Emma became known as "Mae's mom." Without realizing it, Emma had begun to enter the human community.

When Emma attempted to get her job back at the veterinary hospital, her boss told her he no longer needed her. There was no such thing as maternity leave then, or if there was, she didn't know about it.

Emma felt betrayed. She had been loyal and held his business as if it was her own. Emma thought about the many ways she had supported the clients, their pets, and the business.

Without being asked, she had organized his finances, paid the bills, ordered supplies, cleaned cages, swept and mopped the floors, and did the X-rays when they were needed. She figured out quickly that he was spending more than he was making and made it her job to discover where to cut costs. She realized which advertising schemes weren't working. She built rapport with clients by making them feel special when they walked in the door. To her, they were like the wounded raptors, with wounded pets, and she tried to be a smiling and calming presence. Maybe more so, to help their pets!

Somehow she knew that many of the pets' problems were the people's problems, but no one wanted to talk about it. She'd learned this a long time ago. At this point, she didn't bother much to try to change the human's mind. She spoke silently to the animals, assuring them she heard their calls for help and would do what she could to get their humans to listen.

She treated every client as a special person and always asked them how they had found the vet clinic. No one had done that before. She started a process of sending thank-you notes and doing check-ins on people's pets.

When she was in premature labor with Mae, the clinic staff didn't know how to run the clinic without her. They sent in the vet's girlfriend to ask Emma how the finances were run, how they ordered the pharmaceuticals, and even how they scheduled clients.

She thought she had done a good job throughout her time at the veterinary hospital. Yes, she was just a young woman and only had a bachelor's degree, but she knew she was more than that in her heart. She knew she had helped his business. But there was a great divide between being a young woman and being a man. She felt it. If she had tried to say anything about it, she knew it would have become a battle of wills.

For the first time in her life, she understood she was replaceable. She had seen this happen in nature when a lead mare gets injured and the herd pushes her out. Although she felt the pain of being excommunicated from a job that held great meaning to her, there was nothing she could do to change it.

Emma realized she was lacking in her human relations. She didn't feel like she could take a stand for herself. While she was a good mama bear protecting her babe, she still felt awkward maneuvering in the human world.

"What would be a good thing I could do to get more comfortable with humans?" she wondered. "A waitress would be good because then I would need to have lots of superficial conversations. I could work lunches while Mae takes her afternoon naps at my friend's house."

Being a waitress and cleaning houses allowed Emma to be with her daughter while she practiced human skills. She liked serving people and taking care of them. She knew she could go to the city if she wanted to and make good money, but she wasn't willing to put her daughter in daycare.

Emma and Mae's father began to grow apart. He felt threatened by her independence. His childhood scars were like ghosts that came out of the closet and haunted him. He wouldn't talk about his past, yet looking at his baby girl brought back something horrible that took him down a destructive path of self-defeat. Emma tried to save him. But she could not. Emma had to save her baby girl and knew she needed to give Mae a better life. So, Emma left her husband and moved into a small one-room apartment below a rundown house on the outskirts of Petaluma. Mae had the bedroom, and Emma slept on the futon couch in the kitchen.

Living for the next twenty-dollar bill wasn't a secure way to raise Mae. Emma decided to go back to school and tend to her career. She was accepted to graduate school at San Francisco State University to get her master's degree in biology.

She chose to specialize in the ecosystem of the Petaluma River. Part of her research included doing numerous research studies that would require being gone in the wee hours of the morning or late into the night to study nocturnal wildlife patterns and population density. As the time got closer for her to start school, Emma realized it would be virtually impossible to find a babysitter at such uncommon hours. So, she made the hard decision to decline her acceptance. The professor was disappointed, but Emma knew this was her only choice.

She took the next obvious route and applied for full-time work at a horse ranch, training horses and managing the stables. She was quickly hired due to her strong work history and experience with horses. She loved being with the horses all day while Mae played at a new outdoor preschool.

Emma painted the twelve-stall barn, cleaned stalls, fed the horses, and even built a road through the back pasture. One afternoon, she sat in the shade under an old oak tree, exhausted.

"Gosh, now I know how guys feel. I just want to go home, put my feet up, and do nothing. But Mae is waiting for me to come home and play with her."

"Why are you working so hard?" whispered the old oak.

"Because it's the only thing I know how to do. And I'm good at it."

"Yes, but you are a mother now, and it's time to start being a woman. It's time to stop proving you can work as hard as a man. Mae needs your love and support. This job sucks all the energy out of you, and there's not enough left for Mae. It's time to stretch yourself out of your comfort zone. What else are you good at besides hard physical labor?" the old oak challenged.

"I'm a good artist. Hmm, maybe I can make that into a career." She looked up into the oak's canopy of protective leaves and said, "Thank you for standing for me and helping me see my next path." And with that, she went home to Mae with a new spark of excitement for her future.

Knowing she couldn't immediately create art to support herself and her child, she found a full-time job as an executive secretary and had to wear dresses to work for the first time. She promised herself she would stay at the job for one year to add a new skill to her resume. It was fun to pretend she was a city girl. She watched how the other women dressed and the kind of shoes they wore. When she came home from work, Mae would put on her high heel shoes and walk around the house like she was all dressed up to go to town.

"You are so fancy, silly girl." Emma laughed with a deep love for her child.

At work, Emma supported the president and vice president of a medical records product business. The three of them worked in a building across the parking lot from the main building, where the rest of the employees were. Most of the time, Emma was in the large six-office building by herself. It reminded her of having her own tack room away from the other people.

"I wonder why that always happens?" she considered one day, looking out the floor-to-ceiling window in front of her desk. She didn't mind working alone; she was used to it. Sometimes there wasn't much to do, so she would draw and imagine a career in art. Not the starving artist type of career, a professional career.

One day, her boss was interviewing a graphic designer to design a catalog for their file products. Without another thought, Emma set her intention to become a graphic designer.

She convinced her boss to let her go to San Francisco one day a week to study graphic design at the Academy of Arts, which she began to do almost immediately. She told him she could apply her new skills to the business as it expanded. Her boss not only agreed, but he also bought her a drafting table and asked her to draft up some product designs.

One of the other employees, named Kim, became threatened by Emma. Her boss told her that Kim had come to him and expressed her fear that Emma would take over her job. Kim had been with the company for twenty years, and he felt loyal to her.

"I'm going to make a new position for you as the graphic designer for the business. That way, Kim won't feel like something is being taken away from her," her boss confided in her.

"Thank you! I can't wait to start." Emma smiled and felt acknowledged for her skill.

Reality took a sudden turn at a staff meeting her boss convened. He started the meeting by discussing the new position he had created. Kim was sitting across the conference table from Emma. The air in the room suddenly became stuffy, as if everyone was holding their breath to find out who was going to get the new position. Emma smiled to herself, waiting for him to say her name.

"I've decided to give the new position to you, Kim," her boss said and looked away from Emma and spoke directly to Kim. Emma's heart missed a beat. He had told her she had the position, yet he had changed his mind and given it to Kim without any forewarning. Emma felt betrayed, lied to. After that day, she became sullen and moody. She didn't trust her boss anymore and wasn't proud to be of service at the company.

"What is wrong with you, Emma?" her boss asked insistently one afternoon when he came back from a business lunch.

"I'm hurt that you gave the position to Kim and not to me."

"Yeah, but you know I did that because she has seniority over you, and she decided she wanted the position," he said defensively.

"You could have told me before the meeting. It really hurt me that I found out I didn't get the position I thought I had earned in front of everyone. It's like everyone knew but me. I felt like the emperor with no clothes," she said in a tight voice.

"Emma, I can't handle your attitude. You are fired," he declared.

She stood and faced him head-on, "No, I quit!"

She cleaned out her desk and left in tears.

Emma was determined to move forward and prove herself as an artist. She completed her studies in graphic design. She joined the local Business and Professional Women's Club and the Chamber of Commerce. She sold notecards at the neighborhood bookstore and her artwork at nearby horse shows and other summer and holiday fairs.

Her small graphic design business started to take off. She brought Mae with her to client meetings, which turned out to be a great idea because Mae easily opened social conversations for Emma.

As Emma started to prove her success as an artist and designer, her self-confidence grew. She felt good about herself, and she was doing something she loved. She could do her artwork at home while Mae played nearby.

Once a week, Emma and Mae drove down to Sausalito to visit her mom. Since the divorce after twenty-five years of marriage, her mom had become very depressed and was often suicidal. Emma was worried about her mother driving alone to Petaluma for her weekly therapy sessions, so Emma started to pick her up, take her to therapy, and drive back to Petaluma.

Her mother's therapist, Ken, lived on a small ranch west of the town of Petaluma. Emma loved this part of the countryside, which was still dairy country. Little did she know that he would become her husband one day.

After her mother's session, he'd ask Emma about the raptors flying overhead since he knew that had been one of her specialties at Davis. She often wondered if he was really curious about the birds or if he was flirting with her. He was quite charming, but he was also quite a bit older than her.

Their interest in one another grew, and six months later, they started dating. One thing led to another, and a year later, Emma moved herself, her horse, dogs, cats, and baby girl to his place in the country. For the first time, she had her own place where she could stretch her wings and live with her horse. She spent time with the raptors as free spirits rather than wounded birds in rehabilitation centers.

Emma bought a few more horses and went into business training horse and rider. She particularly enjoyed rescuing racehorses off the track and retraining them as jumping horses. Her horses lived in a field that surrounded the old barn that had been transformed into an aikido dojo where people came to study.

This was a new experience for Emma having people come to her home space several times a week. The aikido and somatics students had to drive between the house and the horse barn and often drove too fast. Emma worried they would run over one of the animals or, worse yet, her daughter as they hurried from the house to the barn. Ken's students were free to walk into her home and often found her in her secret garden, in the horse barn, or riding in the arena. Sometimes she had no privacy, nowhere to be alone, and no place to hide.

She felt bad when she didn't want to socialize with Ken's students. She admired his gregarious nature and ease with people. In contrast, she still felt quite awkward with people. She noticed that she was more relaxed with people when horses were around or when she was in the garden with them. She observed how her horses were different with different people. The horses seemed to be interested in some people, while others caused the horses to pin their ears back or try to bite.

Emma was sitting on the back of Cairo, her grey Arabian gelding, on the day she had an epiphany that changed her life. The sun was beating down on the quiet, dusty arena. The surrounding fields were golden brown. Emma looked to the far horizon as she heard a deep voice whisper, "You know, Emma, you are still avoiding the human world." It was the voice of the great Mother Earth herself.

"So what?"

"Well, you know, if you don't interrupt yourself, you will be like a lone shaman. You will not live into your destiny."

"That sounds perfectly fine to me."

"It is not good enough to shy away. The animals need you; the plants need you; I need you. You are our voice. You have to guide the people back to their animal instincts so they can learn how to be more respectful."

"How am I supposed to do that? Humans don't listen. They don't understand."

"I don't know. That is what you will have to figure out. If you listen to the animals, they will teach you how to find your voice. The horses can be your guides. They will show you how they communicate to the human without words."

"But I don't like people very much. They are not honest. They are full of rules about who I should be and how I should act. They think one thing in their mind and say another with their words. They even smile when they are angry. They are so confusing."

"That's not the point. I'm not saying for you to be like them. I'm saying to bring your animal ways into the world of people. You know that what happens to polar bears happens to man. You know that the red-bellied salamander is one of your brothers. How do you teach this to humans? I know you can learn to give voice to how we are all interconnected."

As the sun pressed down on Emma's back, she let her body sink into Cairo, whose shiny white mane flopped over his dapple-gray coat. She held herself close to him, held on tight to his neck, too scared to let go. Cairo stood still like a rock. Emma remembered RT17 and Smiley. She saw the polar bears playing in the snow. She took a deep breath and let out a sigh as a black-shouldered kite hovered nearby. After a long time went by, she slowly sat back up again.

"Okay, I will go back into the world of people and bring my listening with me. I know we humans are out of balance. I do want the polar bears to survive. I do not know if I will succeed, but I will follow your guidance. Thank you."

Mother Earth thanked Emma and blew her a kiss carried on a warm breeze from the ocean.

The Horse Calls Me

The horses call me
Whinnying their words of wisdom
Asking me to listen
"Listen deeply," they say, "to the earth's pulse within you."

In turn, the horses listen to my stories, my fears, my imaginations
They wait patiently for me to return to my own beginning
As I walk among my animal brothers and sisters

Where did all the people go?
How long ago did they lose their way?
Why have they forsaken their earthly dues?
Their allegiance to the interrelations of all life?
Can they change their self-centered ways?
What will it take to heed Earth's call?
What will it take to surrender their brilliance?

Instead, the two-leggeds rape and pillage the land,
Deforest sacred grounds,
They build towns and cities in deserts
And places not meant to be lived in
They ignore the extinction of their plant and animal relations
They don't care enough about the poisoning of the earth's soil

And in less than one hundred years of mass consumption
People have become a species of fat, unhappy, ungrateful
animals who now have to wage war on each other for more
territory, more oil, and ultimately more consumption.
What happened to living simply?
What happened to drinking water from the stream?
What happened to raising children on home-cooked meals?
What happened to the red-legged frog?

The horses call to me now
They ask, "What do you stand for?"
"What will it take to re-awaken man and woman
So they can return to their ancient knowing?
How long will it take until they remember that we are all connected?"

Opportunities and Contemplations

REFLECTION

Entering back into the human world was scary. Having my first daughter forced me to look at my future because now it was about how I needed to take care of her. What kind of mother would I be?

The epiphany I had while riding Cairo was life-changing. It was one of my own equine-guided moments. My path in that instant was clear, and I said "yes" to the beginning of my career in equine-guided education. I made a promise to myself to come back into the world of people, bringing the animal way of communication with me. It was also my promise to RT17, the polar bear, and the natural world to find a way to teach others about their sacred ways.

STAYING PRESENT IN TRYING TIMES

Below are a few questions to inspire some journaling:

- Have you or do you feel undervalued or not recognized for what you offer?
- Was there a time when the world seemed to get out of hand? So many responsibilities, so many things to be done. How did you handle it? What stories did you tell yourself to justify and make sense of it all?
- Is there a new story you would like to write now? If not, let your current story unravel in the pages of your journal as if you are sharing it with a friend.
- How might you think about a new set of criteria for who you are and what you choose to be responsible for?

- What priorities are no longer as important as they once seemed?
- Who really matters to you?

TIME IN NATURE CONTEMPLATION

Take some time in a natural setting with your animals, plants, and guides. Notice colors and smells that inspire you and awaken your heart. Bring them home with you, if only in your mind.

Allow yourself to be free. Imagine a time of timelessness. A time when there were no obligations or rules. No pressure from social priorities.

Does a particular animal or plant stand out to you that embodies an archetype of the self you are calling in? It could even be a person in your life who has embodied a sense of self-freedom and presence.

Truth and Lies

Emma's relationship with Ken blossomed. She took over marketing and enrolling his programs, doing the finances, and tending the gardens. She weeded the rough grounds, planted flowers, fixed the plumbing leaks, and created an oasis of love around his dojo.

She maintained her own income with her horse training and graphic design business. It seemed like students were everywhere, from the dojo to the arena. The private moments at the ranch became less and less. The phone rang more and more.

Emma tried to fit into Ken's social scene. At first, she wore her favorite cowgirl shirts with flowers, but he preferred her in solid colors. So, she wore solid colors when attending social gatherings in the dojo. She changed her attire from cowgirl to a classy woman look. These clothes were not her style, but she knew how to dress the part from her days growing up, helping her mom host parties for her father.

Ken asked Emma to study aikido and somatics with him. She thought it would be a good way to get exposure to people and their communication styles. It was harder than she thought. She found it excruciatingly scary at times to be so close to people and have so many interactions at once.

In aikido class, one student would practice attacking another student numerous times, and then they would switch. This way, they could take turns defending themselves. Most of the aikido students loved the practice. However, Emma was triggered by people coming at her with their hands held forward, intending to grab her throat.

"I don't think this is for me," she told Ken after class one evening.

"It's good for you. Just keep showing up; it will get easier." And so, she persevered.

The somatics classes were even more intense because they practiced aikido attacks with verbal assaults to purposely trigger each other. The idea was not to let people trigger you or throw you off-center. Emma felt like she didn't fit in. It seemed a lot harder for her to tolerate the exercises than it was for the other students.

On days when Emma felt like she couldn't do another somatics class because she felt too triggered by all the human interactions, Ken encouraged her: "Just go to the dojo and keep trying." She followed his advice because she knew it would be easy to give up. She watched how he was when he was teaching and with people in conversations. She watched how he listened, centered himself, and chose to respond to difficult conversations.

She imagined herself as a horse—or sometimes a bird overhead on a wire—listening to the people talking. She knew people would say one thing with their mouths and another with their body language. She had always seen this. But with recurrence and a lot of inquiry, she learned a different way to respond. Rather than get frustrated with the person in front of her, she learned to separate herself from that person. She practiced listening just to listen.

She made a new game. She imagined people as if they were horses or wild animals. In this way, she saw through the mismatch between the words they spoke and what their body said. She saw the gap between where they were and where they wanted to be. She found she had much more patience and compassion for them when she thought of them as an animal, which in truth, they were.

She began to see how the energy of their body language was a thousand times more communicative than the words they used. She noticed that most people reacted to the energy of what was spoken, expressed through tense shoulders or pursed eyes. She learned to navigate between the worlds of animal communication and human communication at the same time, traveling in and out between words spoken and energy felt.

Body language was always a part of animal communication. But for some reason, most humans didn't seem to listen to or respect the energy of the situation. The ones who did were often socially demoralized because they were the first to call out the elephant in the room.

Emma was like a horse; she felt the untruths, the pretenses. She saw the unspoken assessments, the elephant in the room that no one wanted to talk about. When there was a lack of unity between the human group, she felt unsafe—like a wild horse in a paddock full of crazy humans.

By continually separating the grains of sand between animal communication and human language, Emma learned how to articulate what she observed in the relationship between a person's body language and their spoken words. She learned that she did not track in words; she was more acutely tuned to a person's energy or way of being. This explained why she sometimes felt crazy around people. It wasn't that she was crazy at all. She was extremely sensitive to the human animal's lack of congruence between their words and their body language.

As a human, Emma had been taught to trust what people said as the truth. As an animal, she had been trained to trust the energy of everything around her as the primary source of information and choice. These two worlds were as different as the grit of the driest desert and the sensual moisture of a rainforest. She much preferred the honest communication she felt in nature and with animals. Yet, she remembered her promise to Mother Earth to find a way to bring nature's wisdom to people so they could become more compassionate, less judgmental, and less blaming of anyone who didn't fit into their value system.

The archaic words of her professors, insisting that animals don't feel, drummed through her head. She knew not only that her professors were wrong but that something had to be done about this terrible lie. She needed to navigate within the human world to save her plant and animal kin. She needed to share their stories and speak their truths.

Emma went deep into the forest to find her voice. The task wasn't easy since the plants and animals didn't speak human. But her ancestors guided her along the way. She asked questions of the alders, bays, ferns, and cleavers. She listened. Her imagination was on fire. She could hear the ancient chants of the native people who had lived before her. Everything was connected.

She went out and talked to the horses about her vision to form a bridge of communication between humans and the earth. Maybe they could help her find the words that people could understand.

"How do I describe something that makes complete sense to you and me to people who are too busy to listen?" she asked the horses. "How do I describe it to people who would rather not know, rather not believe that their lives are not limited to the cells in their bodies? Why should they even care? Do you see what I'm saying?"

"Neiggggh!" They whinnied cheerily.

"All right already, are you guys on board if I bring the humans out to learn about their presence by working with you?"

"Neiggggh!" They whinnied louder. "Finally, she's getting the message," they whispered excitedly to each other. They cheerily whinnied some more.

Emma knew people could learn a lot about their own somatic awareness—or lack thereof—by being with horses. Horses were her obvious
bridge to connect people to the larger energy field around them. They
lived and breathed in the energy fields. They relied on their somatic
sensations to gauge safety versus danger.

Plans and agreements were made. Emma cloaked her vision in words
humans could understand: "Leadership Development and Somatic
Sensibility."

Her first programs were Leadership, Somatics and Horses™ and
Somatic Horsemanship. She invited Ken's aikido students, leadership
and somatics students, and her riding students to learn about the power
of nonverbal communication from the horses.

Emma didn't expect what happened next. The life-changing perspectives of humans in the presence of horses were quick, dramatic, and

undeniable. The horses became her voice without words. They spoke with their body language. They mirrored each person's underlying moods and attitudes and disclosed the gaps in communication that she had experienced through most of her life.

Along with her horse partners, Emma witnessed the lies people told themselves, the lies others had told them, and the lies they told others. Oftentimes, they didn't even know they were lying. But the horses did. Their feedback was direct and frank. For some mysterious reason, her students could take the feedback from horses in a way they would not from other human beings.

Emma didn't even have to say much at all. She watched in awe as the horses rewired the people's energy fields so they could see more, feel more, and find more courage to tell their own truths. Once they were free of the lies (even for a few moments), there was an opening for Emma to connect them to a bigger purpose, a bigger connection to the earth. Her hope was that if they could tap into their instincts, they would be able to see the rest of the animate world all around them.

It became a common confession for people to say, "Oh my gosh, what is happening with the horse right now is what is happening in my real-life situation!"

Deep inside, Emma was not surprised. "Well," she said, "let's work on your real-life situation. Let's see if we can change the way your body language and nonverbal communication are confusing your real-life relationships." And so, her pioneering work in equine-guided education was born.

Most of the time, Emma felt she learned more from the horses than her students did. She was relieved to see the horses respond the same way she felt toward certain people. She wasn't crazy after all. But the horses were significantly more patient, less judgmental, and quicker to forgive and try again than she was.

She became increasingly fascinated with their generosity of spirit, patience, and compassion. She became their dedicated student. She wanted to learn how to let go of her own lies. She wanted to find the courage to tell her own truth so that she could walk the path she knew was hers to walk.

Emma knew she would have to be brave because no one else in her life saw her truth. They didn't see the silent pain mirrored in the welts Smiley had taken under his owner's hand. They didn't see the historic disempowerment and subordination of Woman; the lie that she had to be less so that others could be more. They saw the pretending, the lipstick, the smiling face trying to make everything okay.

Emma had finally found the bridge she needed to come back into the human world. On the other side of the bridge awaited the wisdom of nature: the answers to life and death, with all its unsentimental harshness, love, and magic.

If she could unlock the doors to her own freedom, become her own powerful being who didn't need to fight and claw for her dignity, then she could help others walk over the bridge. She knew this was her purpose.

As she relaxed into her animal skin and gained confidence that she did not need to give up her animal ways to be with people, the other animals began participating too.

The ravens became her guides. They assisted her in deciphering the mixed messages of people, always showing her the energy of the people, the land, and the mystery of where change can happen. They showed her the portal into the past, present, and future. In this place, they said, one can unlock the prison door of their own making.

"Thank you, wise ones," Emma whispered, relieved to no longer be alone.

"We're in this together," they said. "You're doing pretty good. Just don't let it go to your head. Caa! Caa!" They laughed and smiled. This was fun to do together. They were like private investigators in an invisible web of communication. Emma felt supported by her animal brothers. And the Great Mother, in her wisdom, mirrored her support in her weather patterns.

Foxes, rabbits, hummingbirds, bluebirds, gophers, cats, dogs, goats, herons, egrets, pelicans, weird rainbows in the sky, rainstorms, wind-storms—all began to participate. The fields were full of possibilities.

Woman—You

Woman
You
Yes, you

GO

Go now
Do not hesitate
As the sun sets in the west
Over the ocean blue
You will hold true
To your heart's longing
Remembering your own belonging

Take your horse girl in your hand
And begin to walk upon your land.

Opportunities and Contemplations

REFLECTION

This moment in time was a pivotal turning point in my life. I saw the opportunity to blend the things I loved: horses, art, and creativity. And yet, I still struggled with what other people thought of me. What a crazy thought to bring leadership and horses together. Who would believe me? Would anyone sign up? But I had to do it. I was fascinated with the potential. Here I was, proposing something that was not ordinary—and certainly not proven. I had not taken the clearly defined path of a profession, like being a doctor or a lawyer, as I was supposed to do.

I was worried about what my father would think. But the amazing transformations in my participants could not be denied. I was fascinated to see how patient the horses were with the people. They simply weren't judgmental of people. In contrast, I observed my own judgments of people. I wanted to learn how to be more like the horses, to be less judgmental. They have been my teachers ever since. Life with people without judgment and shame is way more appealing.

It took several years of training in somatics to learn how to be comfortable with people. Incorporating the horses into the somatics program was a great way to learn how to overcome my distrust of people. I learned from the horses how to acknowledge that the pain caused by other people's mean words were stories that had gotten stuck in the cobwebs of their minds. They weren't truths at all. In fact, the stories themselves weren't what were important. It was the way people felt about them.

The horses mirrored the energy, the underlying attitudes and feelings associated with whatever story a person wanted to believe. I was the student even when I was teaching. I slowly learned to reinterpret the untruths my mother had accused me of. I started to see they were her stories of me. They were not my stories about who I was.

THE POWER OF CHOICE

- Reflect on a time in your life when you chose your path independent of what others thought.
- Have you done something or wanted to do something that no one else thought you could do?
- What does it feel like to go back to that remembering?
- What would you like to do differently now?
- What are some of the lies you've told yourself that you may have inherited or accepted from another? What is a new, more life-affirming story that helps you reclaim who you are without apology?

TIME IN NATURE CONTEMPLATION

Take some time in nature. Bring your journal and draw a picture of the scenery or even the weather. Don't make it look pretty or to scale. Try some broad strokes, go for the quality of energy you see, and maybe some colors also.

Describe what you see in big bold dramatic words, full-on, with no apology. The words can go on top of the drawing or on a new page.

If you feel like something deep inside of you is stopping you from being free to draw however you like, take out a new page and draw a picture of that character and the words you hear in your mind. Make everything big and bold; take up the whole page and more.

After you have filled three or more sheets of paper, take six cleansing breaths. Look out into the nature before you and tell the space around you who you are and what you are about. What do you see as possible, independent of what anyone else thinks?

Domestication

At twenty-nine years old, Emma became pregnant with her second child. She felt insecure about being a single mother of two children, but she promised this baby she would be her mother. She knew they had a destiny together, and she would not consider an abortion. Ken ultimately married her when she was six months pregnant.

The day before New Year's Eve, Emma gave birth to Lily, her second daughter. Lily brought both a strong feminine presence and her own push into the world. She was confident, and her spirit was strong. Lily reminded Emma of the importance of staying true to who you are in the world, no matter what anyone else thinks. She had a way with animals, but she needed people in a way that Emma did not.

Lily always wanted to be part of the action. She didn't like to play by herself on the floor. She wanted to go everywhere Emma went. In the mornings, while she worked the horses, Emma put Lily in a playpen in the arena, and when she was done, she'd set Lily on the horse's back for a little ride. Lily was so confident around the horses she would sneak into the pasture with the horses. Emma would rush out of the house and gently call her daughter out of the field. Emma quietly thanked the horses for being so gentle with her little girl.

Lily was a good napper, so Emma took advantage of naptime to do her artwork. Mae helped around the house and was a great big sister to Lily. Happy afternoons were filled with Emma, Mae, and Lily dancing in the living room as fairy princesses, full of joy and lightness.

Emma taught her two daughters how to grow food, harvest berries, and care for the chickens, goats, and horses. She loved cooking with them, canning jam, and preparing food for her husband's classes. Her daughters shared her lifeline to the soil. She felt a new meaning to her life, teaching them about the source of their living, connecting them to nature, and inspiring their own creative expressions.

She proudly taught her daughters how to entertain, in the same ways she had been taught: polish the silver, prepare a fine feast, set the table, place flowers everywhere, light the candles, put your love and heart into all your preparations, dress up, and take care of the guests.

It was easy for Emma to connect with people when her daughters were around. She copied their sociability and ease as they engaged with others. Who would have thought her children would be such great teachers? She reveled in their graceful and kind demeanor when they greeted visitors to the ranch.

The girls enjoyed helping Emma make the dojo and surrounding gardens a beautiful symmetry of indoor and outdoor living, complete with flowers, trees, shrubs, rocks, and shells. The horses held a grounded energy in the lush pasture that surrounded the dojo, while Emma and the girls grounded the domestic gardens and interior spaces. A sense of balance was present on the ranch. Even the hawks, owls, hummingbirds, butterflies, and frogs added their essence.

Emma and Ken continued to merge their professional lives. They taught classes together, imagined their future together, and flourished for many years. She admired his teachership and mastery of his subject matter. She focused her attention on building the business around his somatics work and formed an institute so his work could reach far into the world. She hired and managed staff to support the business. The kitchen table in her house became an office during the day. Aikido students came to the house for dinner. Their personal and professional lives spilled into each other.

Getting pregnant with baby number three was easy for Emma. She loved being pregnant. To the outside observer, she never missed a beat as she waited the last few days before her son's birth. She assembled binders for the leadership classes on the kitchen table, made a country dinner, and cared for the livestock and gardens.

Liam arrived on a rainy morning after a long labor. That evening as Emma held him to her breast, she started to cry. Somehow, her ancient self knew she would have to give him to the world of men when he grew up. She would not be able to hold on to him like she could the girls. She wept with a mixture of deep love and sadness that only a mother would know.

For the first few days of his life, Emma rested with Liam in the sunroom while the staff managed the kitchen office. The environment wasn't peaceful, but Emma didn't care at the time. She and Liam were in their own little world of love. He was quiet and shy like Emma. He was a shining light and brought her an internal joy that was indescribable.

From the time he was born, Liam wouldn't let others hold him. So, he stuck to Emma's hip in his early years. While she taught her equine-guided classes, Liam played with army men in the sand. He was all boy. Emma wondered why he was so fascinated with war and the battlefield. He built cities and battle scenes. He played both sides as if he, too, could feel the tension between two different perspectives fighting to reveal a winner and a loser.

In addition to the programs offered at the ranch, both Emma and Ken developed leadership programs for other businesses and traveled several times a year—sometimes together and sometimes independently. It was hard for Emma to be gone from the kids, so she chose to travel only five times a year. Ken, on the other hand, would be gone up to two weeks per month. Emma stayed home with the kids and focused on running the business.

Emma enjoyed growing the business. She enjoyed forecasting how many courses, how many participants, and how to help more people. She could see in her heart that people's lives changed for the better. Not only did their lives change, but they also became more compassionate, grounded people. That worked for Emma's vision of saving the planet. She knew in her heart that is why she felt so committed to the business.

Each year, she not only met her goal of increasing the business by 20 percent but exceeded it. Growing the business was her way of enlightening human beings and providing financial security for her children at the same time. *What could be better than that?*

She also enjoyed managing the money. She was good at mapping out the financial outlook. It reminded her of the special moments in her father's study, writing the household checks when she was a teenager. She felt like she had a purpose and a brief, if fleeting, sense of control of her life. The business continued to grow, and Emma was happy with her success.

Emma smiled with pride when they acquired a new client with a leadership institute who wanted Ken to present his work twice a year at his conferences. It was a sign that they were now seen as professionals with a talent that other organizations wanted in their programs. It turned out to be a scene filled with cliques, and Emma could see the leader, Ted, was bloated with power. He invited Ken to join his leadership development programs as a member.

Over time, Emma and Ken's conversations about their life and their business began to take on a tense undertone. Ken started using jargon he was learning in the leadership course, and it threw off Emma. For the first time in their relationship, he began to ask her when she'd get things done. He insisted on making her promise when she would fulfill tasks that she was designing and implementing. He had never run the business. He had always depended on her to do all of the finances, enrollments, program management, and the office staff training. He had no clue what promises needed to be made about the "what," "where," or "when." Emma was confused by his new attempts to govern how she kept everything flowing. Because of her dyslexia, the unfamiliar words he flung at her created anxiety.

She decided to take the leadership course, too, so she could understand what Ken was up to and how to negotiate with him using his newfound jargon. The more she learned to speak the jargon he wielded over her, the more he became increasingly condescending, especially in front of company. He wanted to be the only one talking. He didn't like it when she wanted to add to the conversation.

Emma did enjoy learning new business strategies in Ted's program. Initially, she thought she could keep her personal assessments about his character separate from learning the material presented in the program. But the more she watched Ted at his conferences and observed how he treated people, the more concerned she grew. More than once, she witnessed him rail into one of his participants until they were totally demoralized and left the room shaken and in tears. She wanted to put herself between them and him and say, "Stop it!" Just like she had wanted to do for Smiley.

She watched silently as one woman after another allowed Ted to belittle their hobbies, their passions that kept their spirit-self free. Instead, they chose to follow the robotic money-driven criteria for success. Betsy sold her horses, and Libby stopped ice skating. Emma couldn't understand why they acquiesced to Ted's demands.

Deep in her heart, Emma knew Ted was a misogynist. He hated women because, in his mind, they had too much power. And he wanted all the power. His wife was a shell of a woman, like a Stepford wife, addicted to anti-depressants. She had no voice. Emma wanted Ted's wife to stand up to him, defend herself, and own her power.

What a cruel twist that an empowered woman could somehow be a threat to the man she loved, the man who relied on her to make babies and hold the house in harmony (or not). This dangerous twist had passed down through generations and lay like smoking embers in the flames of Emma's genetic memory. She had no way of knowing this in a conscious way. But her animal body was attuned to the twisted game she now had to undertake to survive.

The unspoken pattern that some men who loved empowered women but hated them at the same time began to rear its ugly head between Emma and Ken. Meanwhile, Emma pretended it wasn't so, for if she did acknowledge it, she feared that her life would crumble. Instead, she did everything in her power to protect the children from the underlying discord growing between her and their father.

"Did you see the way Ted railed into Betsy? Don't you think that was totally inappropriate?" Emma asked Ken after one conference.

"Not really," Ken said distractedly.

"It made me feel sick to my stomach," Emma responded.

She was surprised that he didn't see what she saw, and it didn't bother him at all. She trusted her husband, but something strange was happening. She felt him pulling away from her. She noticed that he seemed to be aligning more with the female students in their programs than with her. She was his wife and business partner, but she felt unappreciated for her dutiful service.

She first noticed it with some of the advanced students. They came to the house more often during conferences, and they spoke longer after class. The women acted friendly enough to her face, but their friendliness felt disingenuous to Emma. She saw how they adored her husband, and she felt their envy and jealousy wafting silently in the still air of the conference room.

"Can't you see what is happening?" she asked Ken when she had a moment of his time.

"No. I don't have time to talk about it either," he said on his way out the door. "Oh, by the way, when will dinner be ready?"

The more she tried to talk to him about their relationship and express that she felt something was changing, the more he denied it.

Time passed, and the demands of Emma's world increased. She began to struggle with keeping a balance between her husband's life and her own. Aside from caring for the children and being a good mom, she held her husband's work as her highest priority. At the same time, she knew it was important to keep developing herself and her unique offer in the world. While she flourished as an artist and equine-guided coach, motherhood remained the most significant and rewarding part of Emma's life.

On the home front, the tension between her and Ken grew. In the morning, Emma would wake early to get the kids ready for school. She didn't need an alarm to wake her. She cherished those few minutes with a hot cup of coffee before she woke the kids.

"Time to wake up!" She cheerily came into their room each morning, seeing all three children still fast asleep.

Mae got up first and helped the little ones get dressed while Emma went back to the kitchen to make breakfast. Emma placed bread in the toaster and hurried back to the kids' room to check on their progress, ensuring that they were dressed and their hair brushed. As the kids hit the kitchen, ready for breakfast, she'd find that the toast in the toaster was gone. Ken had come along, eaten the toast, and moved on.

The first few times this happened, Emma sighed to herself and put a new batch of bread in the toaster. One morning, though, she had had enough.

"Ken, has it ever occurred to you that I put the bread in the toaster for the kids? I have to get them out the door by eight," she said angrily. *Who does that?* she thought to herself.

No comment.

"How do you think the bread got in there in the first place?"

No response.

"Well, if you insist on eating their toast, can you at least replace the bread you took and ate and toast a new batch, so the kids have something to eat before we have to leave for school?" She was mad now.

Nothing Emma said seemed to matter. He continued to feed himself without regard for the rest of the family. His lack of awareness for feeding the kids happened other times as well. On days when they were getting ready for a daylong family outing, Ken fed himself while she got the kids ready. She made sure they had jackets and shoes while he made himself a sandwich. He didn't make food for anyone else. He then insisted they get on the road, leaving no time for additional preparation.

Sure enough, half an hour down the road, it was lunchtime, and the kids were hungry. So was Emma. When she asked him to stop somewhere so she could get the kids something to eat, he became irritated with her, as if it was her fault the kids were hungry.

Emma tried to figure out a solution. She didn't have time to get the kids ready and make them lunch before Ken was ready to leave the house. She thought it made perfect sense they would be hungry at noontime and couldn't understand why he couldn't see their need.

Emma felt increasingly unsupported and misunderstood by her husband. The more she tried to get his attention, the more distant he became. Sometimes, he got angry at her for no apparent reason. When she tried to stand up for herself, it only made matters worse. More often than not, she gave up trying to speak about her concerns and the gap she felt growing between them.

Ultimately, the beginning of the end happened. Ted had scheduled an important call with Emma and Ken. Emma knew something was wrong, but she wasn't sure what the call was about. She recalled that on the last business homework assignment she had completed, there was a question that asked, "Was this homework relevant for you?" She wrote back, "While I appreciate the homework, it would have been a better return on my investment to focus on my business plan because this homework seems redundant after the previous assignment."

Emma worried, *What could Ted want? Is he upset that I didn't find his homework valuable?*

Emma and Ken sat on the floor with the conference phone in front of them. She felt the rays of sun on her back and grounded herself through the floor, feeling the cool dirt under her house.

"Emma!" Ted screamed through the phone as the call began. Emma's heart pounded as she prepared for an attack like the ones she had witnessed before. Her animal body knew he was going for her jugular, and his goal was to get her angry and defensive. That way, he would win. Even though every cell in her body was saying to run for her life, she took deep breaths and remained calm. She was determined not to let him kick her off-center.

"Emma, you are nothing!" he yelled. "You think you run the business, but you don't. You don't know anything about finances. You are not even qualified to be a secretary. If something happened to your husband, you wouldn't even be able to get a job! You wouldn't even be able to make $35,000 a year!"

He sounded like the devil. Emma felt his horns reaching through the phone and tearing at her heart.

After a long pause and many deep breaths, she spoke. "Well, Ted, I don't accept your assessment," she responded. Her voice was calm, yet her body was on fire.

"You have never been to the institute to see that I do, indeed, run this business. You have obviously not read my work in your leadership class over these last several years to see that if something happened to Ken before this institute was able to transcend him, I would simply start another business. And if I am so low of a person, why have you allowed me to be in your leadership and entrepreneurship program for so many years now?"

Instead of answering, he screamed at her husband. "Ken! You better rope her in! If you don't rope her in, she will run your business into the ground!"

Her husband said nothing to defend her. He simply said thank you and hung up the phone.

Emma's body was still sitting on the floor, but her spirit had disappeared. She felt wrecked. She knew Ted could be ruthless, but she had not expected such wrath. Her body was shaking, and her blood boiled.

"Did you hear the way he spoke to me? This is totally unacceptable. Why didn't you stand up for me? How can this be okay with you? I'm your wife. I'm your business partner."

"I didn't think I needed to stand up for you," Ken replied nonchalantly.

"He just attacked my character in the most unconscionable way. He attacked my whole being. Please call him back and tell him it was inexcusable to talk to your wife that way and that he owes us both an apology," she pleaded.

"I'm not going to do that, Emma."

Instead, he continued to work with Ted. Three weeks later, Ted's secretary, Charlette, called her and asked Emma if she would be signing up for the next year of the leadership program with Ted.

"I don't think I can," Emma responded.

"Can't you just submit to Ted?" Charlette queried, and with that, the hair on Emma's back raised up tall like a wolf's does when it is ready to fight. "No, absolutely not, Charlette; thank you for helping me get really clear that I will not be attending the program again."

And with that, Emma hung up the phone. She was shaking so hard she could barely breathe. She ran down to the barn to wrap her arms around Sumi and cry.

Ted took the upper hand and told his staff and program participants that Emma was out of integrity and had to be expelled. Ted also told his staff never to speak to Emma again, even though she had been their direct contact for scheduling. Emma tried several times to ask Ken to stand up for her. She tried to make sense of what was happening. On a walk with her father a few weeks later, she told him, "I don't think I can stay married to Ken if he doesn't take a stand for me with Ted."

"I recommend that you do not make an ultimatum with him. He needs to sort out his relationship with that man on his own," her father responded. Emma was surprised by his suggestion—it didn't make sense. She felt like Smiley being whipped for someone else's pain. She remembered how he stood there and took it because trying to argue against such wrath only makes things worse.

She wanted her father to stand up for her too. She had assumed he would see her point of view. But he didn't, and he was wise, so Emma chose to follow his advice and keep her mouth shut. She tried to suck it up and pretend as if nothing terrible had happened.

What Do You Say In Times Like These?

What do you say in times like these?
When you hear the pain in your silent voice
When the world as you know it no longer exists.

What do you say in times like these?
When the light of the moon glistens on the midnight pond
Shimmering with light and full of hope
While darkness hides around the corner.

What do you say in times like these?
When you know you don't have the answers
You are looking for in the familiar days of yesterday.

What do you say when in spite of it all
The stars shine brightly in the dark of night
Denying your pain
Making you feel alright again?

What do you say when a mother cries
Her heart in pain on silent skies?

What do you say?
What do you say?

Opportunities and Contemplations

REFLECTION

It's taken me years of writing to unravel the deeper underpinnings of this time in my life—to connect the dots.

My children were my pride and joy. But even their happy smiles and delightful laughter couldn't stop my heart from slowly breaking. My confusion over what was happening and why it was happening was a bottomless pit of black nothingness. My pain grew. I felt like a dirty beggar pleading for love and approval and getting kicked in the side instead.

At that time, I didn't fully acknowledge or see clearly that the horses were a mirror of me. I was Smiley, and I couldn't see it. I took it too. But unlike Smiley, my pride hurt. I shamed myself. I felt that I must have done something wrong. I couldn't see the lies; instead, they became truths. I must be the one who is off here. My husband (and my mother) must be right, and I must be wrong. I didn't see yet that I could be myself, in my strength and beauty, even if they held me in disdain. I didn't know how to stand up to them and tell them they were wrong.

I knew that my guilt and shame came from never feeling good enough, never getting it right. Conditioned by the lies my mother told me—that I was lazy and irresponsible or that I looked like a ragamuffin when I was too young to buy my own clothes—I no longer could sort out that the attacks others made on me weren't true. I accepted them as if they were the truth because defending myself was pointless.

I had stopped competing in horse shows by this time because I could no longer train my horses in the subtle yet dominant-subordinate style I had learned. My heart hurt forcing them to do what I wanted them to do when I wanted them to do it. Like I had been trained to do.

Yet, I had allowed myself to become domesticated. Other words for domestication include tame, train, break in, break, master, subdue, belonging to the house, trained to live or work for humans. Wow. I could go on and on here. Yes, I was finding myself professionally in my own body of work, and my efforts were instrumental in growing the business with my husband, but in a sense, the men in my life also wanted to shut me down.

They had a need to tame me further as I allowed my spirit self to come forth—a piece that has threatened men historically. Just like horses had been taught to temper their wild nature through the dominant-subordinate style of training, I was being told to temper my creative, imaginative, intuitive, powerful self. It became even more evident when Ted told Ken to rope me in, to get me tamed or under control. Although I couldn't yet break away, I was beginning to see more clearly that even my father wanted me to stand down at the time.

I was determined to defend and care for my children. Perhaps that is why I put up with such painful disrespect for so long. I had been shaped by a lifetime of psycho-spiritual abuse—both directed at me and what I witnessed in others. It seemed normal to me. I was accustomed to it. The mean girls spitting on that girl in the tack box, my little girl telling them to stop, red-tailed hawks shot out of the sky due to ignorance—I had gotten used to all of it.

I considered further what we've done to animals. We have domesticated horses, dogs, cats, and more throughout our evolution. What are the subliminal messages here? How far back does it go? Women and animals have been domesticated for how long?

My mother's generation was taught to go to college to find a good husband. They were taught how to set a good table for a meal and how to entertain so their husbands would be proud. In my mother's generation, a word of praise went like this: "She's so domestic." Those women were my role models.

Meanwhile, Gloria Steinem was saying to my generation that a woman has more choices. I was caught in between different perceptions of reality. I was caught between generations of domesticated women I respected and women who declared that we shouldn't be disempowered by domestication.

The timeless value of being a good wife and mother was no longer valuable. It was looked down on. I loved being a wife. I loved my children. Inside, I felt that my most important value was wrong. What were the truths, and what were the lies?

HAVE YOU EVER FELT DOMESTICATED?

- What metaphors arise for you? Journal about it. See how you can integrate characters in nature (animals, plants, weather) to describe the mood and feelings of your story.
- Have you become too domesticated?
- What are some of your truths and lies?
- These are perceptions; so, what new story do you want to create for yourself? What new truths?
- What wants to stay the same?
- What wants to change?

TIME IN NATURE CONTEMPLATION

Go outside to a natural environment as far away from people as possible. Notice who greets you there. Find a quiet spot where you feel peaceful and contemplative in nature. Begin a conversation with the beings around you, be it trees, dirt, rocks, birds.

What is the difference between being in nature and being in domesticated environments?

What new perspectives do you have after having these contemplative conversations?

Checkmate

Things went from bad to worse. When Ken came home from a busy day at work, instead of setting up his laptop next to hers on the dining room table, as he had always done before, he moved Emma's laptop completely off the table. He put his computer where hers had been. She quietly watched him do this day in and day out as she cooked dinner for the family.

There had always been plenty of room for both of them. There were twelve seats at the table, after all. What was going on?

Emma didn't know what to make of this behavior. She tried to move his computer over and put her computer back where it had been, but that didn't work. He moved it away again.

A few months later, a friend and mutual student of theirs invited them to her wedding in Southern California.

"Emma, you need to buy your own ticket to the wedding," Ken began the conversation. Liam was playing with his army men on the floor, and Emma was about to get dinner ready.

Emma felt her defiance kick in, like a mare who pins her ears to tell the other horse to stop moving into her space. "That is silly. She is our friend and our student. The company should pay for both of our tickets. "

"No, the company is not going to pay for your ticket, only mine." Emma didn't want the kids to feel the growing tension between their father and her, but it was too late.

Emma was stunned. "This makes no sense at all," she said. "I'm your wife and your business partner."

He became angry and gruff. "No, you are on your own. Pay for it yourself. This is the way it will be," he insisted, and that was that.

At the office, tension continued to grow between Emma and Ken. Emma noticed staff members beginning to whisper in the corners when she walked into the office. One woman, Prudence, continually complained at staff meetings to Ken about Emma. Emma didn't know it, but they were forming a male-female bond that would last beyond her marriage. When Emma tried to defend herself at a staff meeting, Ken goaded her further, resulting in arguments in front of the other staff.

Emma wanted to kick and scream, to run and buck like a wild horse. How dare she be treated so terribly! She had put most of her career into making this business. She created the infrastructure for their business to expand and grow. She managed the finances, payroll, program curriculum development, personnel, sales and enrollment, and customer service. She had created jobs for almost a dozen people. It was up to her to hold them accountable for their work promises. Meanwhile, Ken's sole role was as the master teacher.

As Ken expressed his anger at her in front of the staff, she felt dismissed by the very people she had hired. She could see that the staff felt forced to choose sides because of the tension in her marriage. He was the teacher, so of course, they would choose his side. It didn't matter that the classroom and the office space were two different domains.

One early evening over a glass of wine, Ken said, "It's time for you to focus on your horse business and making more money. The staff doesn't want you in our business anymore. Nobody trusts you."

What? When, how, and why had this great divide begun? How had it come this far?

Emma couldn't hold it all in. Her spirit broke into little pieces and scattered on the kitchen floor. This time, she couldn't put it back together with a smile and some glue. Her heart ached so bad that she was afraid something was physically wrong with her. She took herself to the emergency room, only to find that all her organs were in good working order. It was something else that had broken.

Emma couldn't make sense of what was happening. But the land did. It provided her a place to lie down and cry, a branch to hold onto, and ground so strong she could not disappear within it. The fog rolled in over the field and made a blanket around her so no one could see while she licked her wounds. Sumi stood over her, protecting her from the outer world. Emma's body sunk into the earth, and she fell asleep. She dreamt of her great-grandmothers. She dreamt of the black raven flying free. She dreamt of RT17. He had a new wing, and he was circling above her with his raptor call. "Don't give up, Emma. Please fly with me. I love you, thank you."

The animals and plants were the only ones she could trust. They saw what she had forgotten: she had a deep love and passion that needed to be shared.

"Go forward, dear one," the wind whispered. "We need you now. Dust yourself off, hold your head up, and fuel yourself with my steamy breath."

What Did I Do to Cause Such Pain?

They always seem to show up at just the right time.
The wind whirling its noisy breath in dusty swirls,
The dogs, Rosie and Gracie,
Nudging me as if to say, "Everything is okay."
Angelina, the magical cat, meowing insistently.
All calling me back.

They won't let me hide.
They say, "Your place is here."
"You are our pride."

Even though I don't feel strong now.
I wonder what it is I did.
That started the quarrel.
Maybe I didn't do anything wrong.
Maybe it wasn't my fault.

Maybe I was just being my animal self
Feeling my way through a human world,
Full of its judgment and pretense.
All I know for sure is that the wind
Continues to whirl,
The fog rolls in and covers me like a blanket,
The night becomes dark.

I hope tomorrow I will awaken
With fresh eyes, a clear mind
And a heart open to seeing things anew.

Opportunities and Contemplations

REFLECTION

There's a lot more to this part of the story, but suffice it to say, I felt like I was going crazy. Reading this poem, after all these years, I know I continued to try to figure out what I had done wrong. Yet, I couldn't figure out why my husband was angry with me.

I was never able to figure out what I had done wrong. I can see all of my successes: a business in his name that still thrives, three beautiful children, the books I've written, the people who still write to me, even twenty years later, and state how "that day with the horses" changed their lives. But I couldn't and still can't see what I did wrong.

Looking back, I can see people like Prudence, who wanted to oust me from my throne and take away my king. Ted wanted to annihilate my feminine power. I know both Ted and Prudence turned Ken against me. They had a need for power to such a degree that they needed to take it away from me. What I have never been able to understand, though, is why my husband didn't stand up for me and protect me.

I understand with my entire being that what this trio of people did to undermine the foundation of my identity was evil. After years of deep healing, I can now see that their malicious intent was to attack my character so I would get angry. Then, they would accuse me of being defensive. I often felt like a wild animal trapped in a corner with no way out but to fight for my life. It took a lot to get me there and ended with a sense of humiliation I could not recover from. Once I was angry, they simply pointed their finger at me, smiling, as if to say, "Ha, look at her now. She is so angry. Hahaha!"

During my marriage, I had a recurring vision (actually, it was a visceral experience) of following my husband into a psychological conversation.

When you are in the self-development world like I have been, you can get tricked into thinking that every moment is an opportunity to fix or better yourself. So, in this vision, I follow his lead. He is the therapist, after all. He has the credentials. We are on the edge of a huge dark lake. I follow him into the murky waters. Before I know it, I can't touch the earth anymore, and I am in the middle of the lake. He is still on the shore, and I am starting to drown. I am stuck out there, calling for help, and he is on the shore with a smile on his face. He points his finger at me, "Look at her. I got her once again." I am abandoned in the black waters to save myself. It reminds me of being a little girl with my hands outstretched, crying and asking my mother to pick me up and getting no response.

The healing work I've done has served me well. I don't get trapped in the corner any longer. No one can take advantage of me in this way anymore. The visual of me drowning in the lake with him on the sidelines laughing was the first step for me to start listening to my animal body. Shortly after this period of time, I no longer trusted him to go to the metaphoric lake. That was the beginning of finding a new way to set myself free. Fighting and defending myself were not the gateway to my new green field full of possibilities.

One thing I have learned from all of the hard work I have been present to, not only for myself but for those others in my classes who are working to reclaim their dignity, is this: if you can't find out what you did wrong, then most likely you didn't do anything wrong.

This is what makes being human so hard for me. Sometimes there are people in our life who do not have our best interest at heart. They are self-absorbed and focused on gaining power at any expense, even someone else's. I was merely the queen on Ken's chessboard as long as it served him, but he would checkmate me in the end. I was about to be ousted. He had rallied all his pawns to take his side. And I had allowed it to happen.

Why did I stay? I had my children. I believed in marriage. And, most importantly, I was playing a game I could not win, just as I'd always done. After years of journaling, what I can see now is I also placed too much emphasis on the success of his business identity and not enough on my own.

OUSTED FROM YOUR THRONE

Have you ever felt ousted? Can you remember the events that happened before your opponent checkmated you? If the chess metaphor doesn't work, have you ever felt misunderstood, misrepresented, or manipulated by someone else?

Write and journal about it. Have two pieces of paper on the table. Let one be the raw, unedited emotions you feel as you remember. Let the other be the wise woman who has always resided in you. The one who has never let you down. What does *she* look like?

Is the thought of allowing yourself to be the queen of your own dignity hard for you?

If so, rant about it until your emotions are spent. When the emotions have subsided, take a few minutes to let your wise woman stand tall and be a voice that shall not be silenced.

Speak her words to yourself as you look in the mirror. She lives inside you; bring her out to play.

TIME IN NATURE CONTEMPLATION

Go to a park where other people are, if possible. Sit on a bench. Notice the foliage around, the trees, grasses, flowers. Now notice the people. Watch how they relate to each other. Notice how your body feels in response.

Ask your wise woman self: Who am I drawn to and why? Do I want to help someone? If so, why? Do I want to rescue someone? Do I want someone to come to me and say hi? Who feels unsafe? Why? Who is not happy? Who is happy?

Observe the social dynamics between families, friends, and people who walk by. Notice your opinions and let them go. Observe again with fresh eyes.

Now go back to noticing nature around you, perhaps the birds, the plants. What is different in your body now?

Spirit Horse Returns

It was a late night; the children were sleeping peacefully in their beds. Emma turned off her light, wondering what tomorrow would bring. The clean sheets felt smooth as she nestled under the covers. As she fell into that light sleep where the body falls gently deeper into the mattress, something woke her.

She sat up in bed, her body alert. Nothing in her home had changed. Her children were fast asleep. As she lay her head back on the pillow, an old forgotten memory came to her. Without thinking much about it, she quickly turned on her reading light and scribbled down some notes.

Tears came to her eyes, and suddenly, she was young again, back at Tennessee Valley. The memories poured forth, and she saw Golda, the big, sturdy palomino mare with a long, flowing mane the color of pale straw. Golda lived in a stall along the wall of the barn, set apart from the other horse stalls. Day after day, Golda remained in her stall, present to any passerby who bothered to notice the lone horse.

Emma often found herself leaning into the stall, her hand on Golda's neck between the warmth of her soft coat and thick mane. It was as if, somehow, the two grounded each other in their aloneness, confirming the existence of nothing and everything at the same time. An understanding grew between them. Sometimes Emma couldn't remember how long they stood there, speaking to each other in silence. Over time, Golda became a quiet place of acceptance for Emma, and perhaps the lone teenager returned the favor in kind. Only Golda could say for sure.

As Emma sat alone in her bed that late night, tears gently moistened her cheek. She wondered silently, "Why have you come to me now, Golda?"

Golda reminded her of the sadness she felt at the thought of this graceful animal abandoned to confinement in a stall big enough only to turn away from the world and a window large enough to stick her muzzle out to the strangers walking by.

Day after day, Golda remained in the stall. Nobody came to release her—to set her free, if only momentarily—to let her run into the wind, to stretch her running legs. Sometimes Emma imagined sitting on Golda, opening the stall door, and racing down the path to the ocean with the full moon lighting the way.

All the other horses had a human who, at the very least, worried over them, projecting their fears and insecurities onto their stalled horse who had no choice but to listen. Most of the other stall horses were a little crazy, trying various means of shedding their human's pain. Shalom was fiery, unpredictable, and only his owner could ride him. Sheera would try to bite every passerby, teeth bared as if any contact were better than none. Chip always found a way to hurt himself so his human would hire Emma to take care of this injury or that.

Many of the barn ladies hired Emma to take care of their horses in some manner or other. But there seemed to be no human for Golda;

Emma was not allowed to care for her as she did the other horses. Maybe that is why she spent so much time leaning into the big mare's stall when all the other humans were gone. She often wondered why Golda was not crazy like the rest. It seemed unnatural for a horse who was so chronically confined not to have some nervous tick. But Golda was always stoic, peaceful. To this day, Emma could not explain it.

More tears came as Emma recalled the day that Golda's owners came to the barn. The whole family was there: mother, father, daughter, and son. They took the lone horse from her stall, saddled her, and took her to the arena for a ride as if everything were fine and normal.

Ingrained in Emma's memory was the picture of Golda taking these strangers for a ride in full grace and dignity. She rode them around, and around, and around. Never once did she show a sign of resistance or irritation. Her selfless commitment to engaging in their fantasy of owning a horse seemed unnatural. Nevertheless, she rode them around and around.

The people didn't even know that they could ride her too hard. With humans, it is dangerous to take a stalled athlete who hasn't exercised in months and make him run a marathon. The same is true for a horse who has been confined to a stall for too long. The humans' lack of consideration, or complete ignorance, was staggering. And yet, Golda didn't feel a need to talk about herself.

At the end of the day, the family unsaddled the patient mare, put her back in her stall, and left with smiles on their faces. They never came out to the barn again.

On that late night of memories, Emma cried and looked up at Golda, who was now standing at her bedside. "What did you do? What happened to you? The last time I saw you, you were still in the stall. Why have you come to me now?"

"Lay down and rest now, child," Golda replied. "We will talk again." And then she was gone.

What Emma didn't know was, at night, when all the humans were asleep in their beds and the barn was quiet, Golda gathered the spirits of like-minded horses for prayer. Most of the other horses in the barn did not hear her invitations, as they were still caught in the confusion that came with being owned. They had not realized that their spirits could be free, even if they lived in the world of humans who thought that owning a horse somehow gave them governing power over their spiritual lives and animal ways.

Golda had found a way to keep her spirit alive by extending beyond her stall and imagining herself in a green field at the foot of the bay where the salt water from the ocean met the fresh water of the rivers. There were other horses there and, even though the field was fenced, the horses were content. In this field, they could be horses by day and horses by night. They napped in the morning sun and frolicked in the afternoon breeze. They could smell the fresh air off the ocean bringing in distant yet familiar smells. The field was lush with possibility.

For weeks, Emma couldn't get the memory of Golda out of her mind. Her determination to discover what had happened to the majestic horse of her past gained momentum.

She looked into the field of horses and asked, "Why did you come to me now, Golda? What is it you want me to see?"

Sometimes Golda would appear in the silhouette of the big horse named Billy that was in training with Emma. Sometimes Emma could feel Golda's steamy breath on her neck as if to say, "You are asking the right question, dear one."

Every time Golda appeared, Emma welled up with tears. She pretended she didn't know why. She wanted desperately to avoid the conversation Golda had come to have with her. At first, she was excited to see her old friend. She remembered her elegant nature and her sudden disappearance. But Golda seemed serious now. Even the memory of

Golda's isolation and loneliness brought up emotions Emma really didn't want to feel. Every time Emma tried to shy away from feeling into why Golda had come, the mystical horse got larger than life and more insistent.

Following Golda's call meant she had to settle into the unknown and a remembered place the wild ones had led her to many times before. The place where one cannot "know" their way. The place where destiny has no understanding. Without knowing it, Emma felt if she followed Golda's call to attention, she might lose what ground her in the human world.

One crisp, coastal morning, as Emma fed the horses, she found herself leaning into a new horse's stall. The horse had been brought to Emma to try to find her spirit. Her previous owner had abandoned her. She was spiritually void, depressed, and unrideable.

Emma tried every way to find a connection with her, to try to wake her up, to inspire her to live. She felt a wave of sadness overcome her. Golda suddenly appeared. But this time, she was so tall that her mane brushed up against the barn rafters. Emma had to look up toward the sky to look into her eyes. She was not sure she was ready to see what the pale horse had to show her. She sat down on the floor of the barn and wept.

The mare nuzzled her cheek, "It is okay, dear one. Let the tears fall."

Emma couldn't imagine ever telling anyone about this spirit horse. No one would understand. But this horse was an old, familiar friend. Emma trusted her. And so, she cried and cried until all her tears were spent. She cried so many tears that a small stream formed and snaked its way out of the barn and down the valley, through the estero where it met the sea. Egrets and herons came to the shores of the estero and looked at their reflection in the water.

Emma looked deep into Golda's eyes and said, "I am ready to see."

She saw herself in a stall, just like Golda. She had everything she needed to stay alive: food, water, bedding. But she was alone. By day she went to work, and she rode the people around, and she rode them around, and she rode them around. And then she went back to the stall.

"What part of me is stuck in the stall?" Emma asked.

"The part of you that goes to the green field by the bay," whispered Golda, "where the fresh water meets the salty sea. Where you nap in the morning sun and frolic in the afternoon breeze."

"Yeah, but I thought I was taking time to nap and frolic," Emma said.

"You are missing the point." Golda turned her head to leave. Emma begged her to stay.

"Emma," Golda spoke boldly now. "The part of you that is alive, that speaks horse, believes in the healing powers of the land, the water, and the animals, the part of you that understands the mystery—*that* part of you is stuck in the stall. It is up to you to answer your own question. How did *I* get out of the stall?"

That night, when the children were asleep in their beds, Emma snuck down to the barn, opened the stall door, climbed onto the pale horse's back, and followed her trail of tears down the valley, through the estero, to the shores of the sea.

Golda's entrance into Emma's inner world had come as a big surprise, and yet, deep inside, she knew why she had come. The realization that her life was upside down came in a slow onset, a long quiet revelation—like walking through the mud as your boots sink into the earth. You feel the suction building, but you need to keep moving. And then, as you reach to take the next step, your boots become the mud pool itself, and you are in your socks. Wet and cold. No shoes.

For a while, Emma hoped her vision would go away. She hoped she could simply open her stall door and set herself free without confronting the demise of her marriage. Yet, the tension between Emma and her husband continued to grow. She kept herself busy taking the kids to school and attending their after-school activities. When she wasn't with the children, she made herself busy at the barn as long as possible to avoid going home to her husband.

One afternoon, she and Ken sat on the porch overlooking the pond to get caught up with each other.

"I've planned a river camping trip with the kids for the first week in August. We'll be gone for a week," Ken informed Emma.

Her optimism quickly faded, and her heart skipped a beat.

"Well, that week is the week I have my leadership program here at the ranch. Can you make it another time so I can go too?" Emma tried to be accommodating.

"It's the only time my other friends can go," Ken replied.

She wondered if he was doing this intentionally to hurt her. She knew the friends he was referring to were some of his female students, including Prudence.

Summoning up the bit of free will she had left, she raised her head high like Golda did and shook her head. "I really want to go too. This doesn't make any sense to me. If it's a family trip, why don't you pick a time when I am free?"

"No, the kids are already excited to go. I told them all about the trip," he said.

Emma felt alone. She was not being included in the family vacation. She had no say, and Ken didn't seem to care that she couldn't go. It felt more like he had picked the dates on purpose, knowing she couldn't go.

Golda continued to haunt Emma with her penetrating presence. The spirit horse of her childhood pressed into her. "Don't you see, Emma, the dis-ease is in your house. You are a stabled horse like I was. You have no power in your home; you are being disrespected as the mother and the matriarch of your family. You are being ridden like I was, without any regard for the health of your own body and spirit, not to mention the ramifications it will have on your children to grow up seeing you disrespected this way. You ask why I have come. Well, that is why. I know you know that I am a reflection of you now, and that is why I am here to guide you out of this tyranny."

In one of Emma's dreams, Ken was putting bricks on her coffin. She was still alive in the coffin. But the coffin was getting smaller and smaller, and the lid of the coffin was getting harder to open. A few more bricks and Emma would no longer be able to get out. She repeated in silent words, "I will not die over this. I will *not die*."

Her left breast hurt often. She went to the doctor to see if it was her heart that was ill at ease. Or was it her breast? Her semi-annual mammograms confirmed irregular cells in her breast tissue that needed to be watched closely. She ended up in the ER twice in one month in extreme pain, only to find nothing wrong.

Emma rode the hills above the estero, asking the Great Spirit to help her, perhaps to send a sign. "What am I supposed to do? What can you help me see more clearly?"

In her dreams, a spider came. The spider kept biting her breast, making a small pink incision that made Emma itch. At first, she thought the message was telling her she had done something wrong. But then she realized that the spider was trying to heal her. Like the goddess Neith, who is the spinner and weaver of destiny, the spider was catching her in her web. The spider caught her attention and told her to attend to herself; her breasts were the part screaming for her attention.

Spider

The spider is biting my breast.
She is relentless, every day biting my breast.

"Why are you biting my breast?"
"What have I done wrong?"
She doesn't answer.
And then I realize that perhaps she is healing me.
Healing me from the curses of the past.
The war on the feminine principle.
She brings the quiet wisdom of ancient ones
Who know that all is connected.

The spider tells me to pay attention to my breasts.
The dis-ease in my breast is a reflection of the dis-ease in my
Great Mother.

I feel a deep sadness I don't want to see.
I feel the pain of the earth and all her relations.
There is nothing I can do to protect her.
I try to pretend I don't see.

I close my eyes.
I am hanging upside down in the spider's web.
I am stuck; I don't know what to do.
"Do not worry, little girl," she says as she bows her head.
"Indeed, you have gotten lost in your own web, my dear.

But remember, the spider does not want her web to be perfect.
The mistake she makes becomes a small tunnel of light so she
can find her way out of the dark.
Remember where I bit you on your breast?"

As she busily weaves her web, she looks down at me and says,
"Do not be afraid of the message," she says.
"Walk on my threads, and you will find the tunnel back into
the light."

She leaves me alone. Upside down.
I fall asleep. It is black all around, but the trees are singing.
I listen.
"Sit by the fire with your family and tell stories.
Listen to the sound of the grasses moving in the breeze.
Stop buying the colorful packages full of waste.
Stop listening to the politicians and corrupt corporations
Who dominate you through fear and scarcity.
Don't listen to their lies.

Everything you need is at your feet.
Take your shoes off and feel the earth talking.
There you will find the simplicity of living.
Find the butterfly who is waiting to be seen."

And the song ends, and I am alone again in my dream.

Opportunities and Contemplations

REFLECTION

Golda *did* come to me. She was persistent and forced me to look at her and listen to her message. She was yet another example of a domesticated being, a prisoner in a dominant-subordinate partnership. She was resilient like Smiley was. I cried so many tears writing this essay because I finally knew I could no longer turn away. My life was at stake.

This is actually the first essay I wrote. I wrote it about a year before I filed for divorce. My friend and colleague had asked me to write a chapter for her book. I saw it as an opportunity to delve into my subconscious. The power of Golda's message ultimately spurred more chapters to try to unwind myself to my beginning, so I could find the strength to reclaim my freedom. I wrote the spider poem around the same time but did not connect the dots until I was diagnosed with breast cancer for the first time a few years later.

My intuition was calling out for me to see, to be my own witness, through journaling and illustrations. Only years later, by going back through these interior reflections, did I see these strong correlations.

I still cry when I read this story. I was Golda, riding people around and around, trying to make everyone happy, and putting my spirit in the stall to keep the peace. My own freedom was still an illusion, but I didn't see it. My kids were thriving. But inside, I was in terrible pain. My spirit was screaming. I wrote this essay to try to understand what she was trying to tell me. And at the same time, I didn't want to look at what Golda was asking me to see.

Deep down, I knew I was upside down, but I didn't want to look at my failing marriage. My main goal in life was to be a good wife and mother.

Why in the world would I want to look in my spirit mirror and admit I was dying inside? Or even worse, I was failing at the one thing I wanted to be good at. Everything looked great on the outside of my life. But my spirit was stuck in the stall.

I felt like I had no one to talk to. I felt like I needed to protect my husband's identity. Yet, I knew that bottling up my emotions and ignoring spirit's call was dangerous.

The intrusive dream of me in a coffin was my ultimate wake-up call. At first, I thought, "Well, I can still lift the lid and get out." Really? I say to myself now. Really? You were okay with that?

Golda brought me the vision of myself stuck in the stall and the opportunity that I was the only one who could set myself free. It was up to me to say no to "coffin life," open my stall door, and set myself free. I thank her presence for starting my journey to reclaim my dignity.

ARE YOU HOLDING BACK
Your Authentic Self?

- Are you stuck in a stall? Explore this question in writing.
- What is the courageous conversation you need to have with yourself before your physical body breaks down?
- Is your body asking for your attention and love?
- Is there someone else you need to have a courageous conversation with?

TIME IN NATURE CONTEMPLATION

Take a few hours—or better yet, a weekend—and spend time in nature several times each day. Find a place to sit that feels comfortable. Sit on a blanket, bring tea for two. Set a place for your spirit self. Sit down and have a conversation with your spirit self.

Ask your spirit self, "What would you like to share with me? I promise I will let you speak, and I will not interrupt you."

Journal, draw. Let your spirit notes be in larger, creative strokes.

If you notice your self-judgments or your "Yeah, but...," "I can't because...," "What about...," you may write them down in very small, tight writing. Keep them in a separate area from your spirit notes. Confine them to a limited space. Don't deny them, just limit their space. If they need to fill the whole page, let them; but make their words small or your columns narrow.

A Vacation from Reality

Every winter, Emma's husband took Emma and the kids away from the ranch for a vacation. He loved to travel, as documented by his well-stamped passport. But Emma preferred to stay rooted. She was quite content to travel ten minutes down the coast to her favorite ocean shores. She loved to remember the secret forays to the beach on Sumi at night or the afternoon romps up the steep trails to the top of Mount Tam.

It was hard for Emma to leave the ranch for extended periods of time, especially in the middle of winter when her flock was lambing. She worried about the baby lambs being born in the heavy rains, being wet too long, and getting pneumonia. She wouldn't be there to rescue them. She worried about bad winds taking down the barn. The cowgirls that offered to stay at the ranch in her absence had numerous tales of animals dying when Emma left. They had each been humbled by Mother Nature's ruthless storms. This time, they vowed that no animal would die while she was away.

Emma asked her husband if they could go a little later in the spring so she could shepherd her flock through the hardest part of winter. But it was the cold he wanted to escape. Emma knew she could not avoid her husband's desire for warmer weather, so she agreed to a week in Mexico. On a wintery Friday morning, the whole family woke before dawn and headed to the airport as the rain beat diligently against their windshield.

As Emma stepped off the plane under the sunny skies of Mexico, her phone rang. It was Gwen. A ewe was down, and the lamb orphaned. Gwen asked Emma what to do.

"Sometimes the older ewes are too weak to make it through a bad storm," Emma said. "Focus on the baby now. Put the lamb in the bathtub under a red heat lamp and feed it some of the milk replacer we have for the orphaned lambs in the barn."

Gwen laughed. She had never heard of a lamb in the bathtub before. It made sense in a ranch kind of way.

Emma recalled that every winter, Ken would say in a gruff tone, "No lambs or baby goats in the house this winter."

"Okay, honey," she would reply sweetly, knowing full well that if a baby needed rescuing, it was coming in the house.

Confident that her instructions had calmed Gwen's nerves, Emma hung up the phone. She hoped that Gwen didn't feel too bad about losing the ewe. Emma wished she hadn't left the ranch, but she wanted to be with her family. She hoped that time with her husband would help heal things between them.

As they drove down the Baja coast, Emma imagined riding along the scruffy landscape, through the washes, past the tall cactus. She remembered the story of a woman from Malibu who had bought a fancy eight-foot-tall cactus to decorate her home. One day, the cactus started to tick like a time bomb. She called 911. The rescue team arrived shortly and shouted, "Get out of the house right away!" She turned and ran out the front door.

Indeed, the cactus was about to explode, but not because a bomb was inside. Rather, thousands of baby tarantulas were about to emerge. Apparently, these cacti were great breeding grounds for the giant spiders, and they make an incredible ticking sound before spewing out the next generation of tarantulas.

Emma shuddered, shaking off the mental image. She watched as the dust from the pale dirt rose behind the car, leaving a silent trail that honey-bees delicately followed. She saw a lone horse hidden in the scrub brush where there were no fences to be seen. The taxi sped on as she looked longingly out the rear window after the horse. She wondered if it was wild.

Further down the one-lane highway, Emma saw a paddock full of dark horses on the beach. She liked the idea of living in a hut on the beach with her horses. *I could live in Mexico if I could live here, away from the tourists*, she thought. The sun warmed her face as she looked out to the ocean, the window down, her hair blowing in the wind.

The kids went directly to the pool once they'd settled into their room. Emma was relieved to find that their room was on the ground floor, looking out at the ocean. The sand was only a few steps away, and a bare patch of earth stretched along a good half a mile of coastline. *I can relax here*, she mused.

Her son, Liam, was thrilled that a giant cruise ship was anchored on the ocean's calm waters. He loved ships. "Do you think they have enough lifeboats?" he asked.

"I think they learned their lesson from the Titanic," Emma replied. "So yes, I think they must have enough."

"What about that one over there?" Liam pointed to another ship.

"Yes, I think they have enough lifeboats," Emma smiled.

"Now, if you were Captain Murdock," Liam said, pointing to the big ship, "and you were driving that cruise ship, what would you do if you saw the iceberg coming?"

"I would drive straight into the iceberg," Emma replied, wondering if she had answered correctly.

"No, no, no," Liam said, shaking his head. He knew more about boats and icebergs than she did. He went into a lengthy explanation of exactly what she should do if she were Captain Murdock about to hit an iceberg with the giant ship in front of them. Emma smiled. A deep, satisfying warmth settled around her heart.

Everyone joked that Liam was going to grow up and be the next Titanic expert. He was obsessed with the Titanic movie. He watched it over and over. Emma watched it with him, not sure why, but she was fascinated with what he was fascinated with. He loved to watch the beginning when all the women, dressed in their best, walked up the planks onto the boat and waived at those left behind on the shores. He loved the romance with Rose and Jack, two passengers from different social classes who fell in love aboard the Titanic during its ill-fated maiden voyage.

And to top it off, he was riveted during the final scenes when the boat was sinking. People were either falling off the boat into the freezing waters or being saved by the few lifeboats that had been secured to the Titanic, more for effect than function.

Liam studied the big picture books about the Titanic and other ships. Emma learned a lot of information from her son, including the fact that over forty thousand eggs had been stored on the giant ship to feed the hungry passengers. She wondered how much space all those eggs must have taken up, who had counted them all, and how many days it must have taken to stock the eggs on the ship.

The sand outside their room called to Emma. She opened the sliding glass door, walked over the wooden bridge, and took the few steps down to the sand. The sand was warm, coarser than her beach sand, but still familiar. A huge brown pelican captured her attention. The pelican's webbed feet hit the ground in a rhythmic pattern. The bird came toward her, and Emma was struck by her tremendously sloped beak, her soft eye. She had never seen a pelican this close before.

But something wasn't right. She looked closer and saw something very large trailing behind the majestic bird. Emma realized it was her wing. The pelican was dragging her left wing—all six feet of it.

Emma tried to put her heart back into her chest. This beautiful bird was *so* damaged. Emma knew she was walking toward her death.

She imagined scooping the bird up in her arms and taking it … where? *Where can I take it?* she thought. There must be a zoo or a rescue center. She struggled to imagine any possibility. If she were home, she could take care of it herself. But now, all she could see was this bird walking around and around while Emma wasted time wondering what to do next.

She ran up the steps to find someone, *anyone*, to help her. She turned back and looked at the bird, who had now come right up to the steps as if to follow her. She looked down at the pelican and saw her shoulder shaking in pain. The bird looked right into Emma's soul, blinked, and asked, "Is there one god or many? Or none at all?"

All Emma could say as she spoke softly to the bird was, "It's okay."

Then to herself, she said, "Really! That's pretty lame. It's not okay. It's fucking not okay." And she broke into tears. She turned away slowly so the bird could not see the tears rolling down her cheeks. She felt at such a loss. Many times before, she had been able to catch a seagull and cut the fishing line from its legs and free it from some human's thoughtless trash. This time, she knew there was nothing she could do.

She went to the concierge of the hotel and explained the situation. "Is there a zoo or humane society that could rescue the bird?" she asked.

The hotel staff promised to take care of the bird and made it clear that they did not need or want her help. Emma knew that their words were empty. She went back to her room, her head hung low, her heart heavy in anguish. Perhaps this was how Gwen was feeling about the ewe she couldn't save.

That night when the kids were sleeping, she got out of bed and scribbled down a poem.

The next day, Emma, her husband, and the kids walked along the beach to the local town of Cabo San Lucas. She looked in vain for the wounded bird who had captured her heart but found no signs of her. Liam continued his barrage of questions about the cruise ships, their lifeboats, and what could have saved the Titanic.

When they got to town, Emma was pleased to see so many healthy pelicans. But she still ached at the tragic outcome of her winged friend further down the beach. She took so many pictures of the pelicans sunning themselves on the tourists' boats that Liam finally grabbed the camera and said, "Mom, I think you've taken enough bird photos."

Emma attempted a smile and distracted herself with the names of the various yachts and fishing boats until the family meandered back down the beach. She avoided looking up at the parasails. The human's desire for entertainment—the next daring adventure—had a cost. Just like the passengers on the Titanic stepped aboard the bold ship, thinking that it was unsinkable. Human error easily betrayed their arrogant beliefs. The human's egotistic notion that will and intellect can defy nature failed in a deadly fashion.

Like bad weather is to humans, humans are to the earth—unstoppable, destructive, and unavoidable. Emma wondered about the unanswerable, indefinable complexity of life.

"Grandmother," she whispered into the ocean waves. "I, too, am abusing the cycle of nature by boarding a plane and flying to a faraway place to vacate my responsibilities. I, too, am contributing to the pretense that we are in balance with our surroundings. I am one of 'those tourists,' even though I won't parasail. I am sitting on the beach, sunning, while the inequities of the world push on."

Emma felt a deep sense of guilt that she was out of balance with the interconnectedness of all things. And yet, she felt helpless to step outside of the rat race and change the course of things. She didn't know how to stop the cycle of humans abusing nature.

Her internal conflict was interrupted by a horse galloping with a handsome dark-skinned cowboy on his back. "Look at the horse coming down the beach," she said to Liam. As the man and horse approached, the cowboy stopped in front of them and gracefully pulled his horse into a bold rear. The horse's front hooves pawed the sky right in front of them, and the cowboy took off his hat, placed it to his chest, and said, "Good day." And without another word, he galloped off.

"Oh, I wish I could do that right now," Emma mused as she watched him disappear into the sandy horizon. She pictured herself atop the sweating animal but stopped short when she imagined her frilly skirt and bare legs mixing with the horse's sweat.

The horse reminded her of home. The cowboy made her smile. She wondered if a storm was pelting the fields around her house and if any more lambs had died. Then, she remembered she would be home soon and, once in her natural surroundings, she might have a better sense of how to be in this complex world.

The next day, she and Ken were sitting on the beach together. Although their bodies were close, the distance between them was vast. Emma asked him in a quiet voice, "Do you want to be married to me anymore?"

Suddenly the sand that had been trilling little fairy dances at her feet stopped its whirl as every grain of sand paused to hear the answer.

"Well, I'm done with parts of the marriage," he stated simply as if he were commenting on the daily news. Emma's heart fell into the sand, her chest suddenly an empty cavity. She told her lungs to fill the emptiness. The sand filled its lungs with air and held her up so she could lean into its bravery.

"Ohhhhh-kayyyy," she spoke slowly. Surprised but not *really* surprised, she asked, "What parts of the marriage are you done with?"

A thousand thoughts raced through her mind. *Why have you not spoken of this before? You sound like you have known this for a long time. Maybe I really am feeling you withdraw? Oh my god, it's worse than I thought! What have I missed? What do you mean PARTS of the marriage?*

"I don't want to be financially responsible for you and the children anymore," he stated matter-of-factly.

The grains of sand began to whirl and twirl in Emma's mind. *How can this be? How can he not want to be responsible for the kids?* Besides, has he forgotten all of Emma's hard work to create their financial security? Once again, she considered everything she had done: she was the one who had created the business, the infrastructure, the marketing, the customer interface, and even the course curriculum around his work. Since they first met, she'd even begun to bring in her own source of income separate from the company.

"I don't understand what you mean," she stated as she silently thought, *There must be way more to it than this.*

"I want free time to travel when I want to and things like that," he said.

"We have the financial security to travel when you want to. It's already in place. I can take on the responsibility of running the company like I used to do. That way, you can take all the time you need to do what you want," Emma offered because she did want him to be happy.

"No. The staff won't follow you," Ken insisted.

"The staff used to. I hired every one of them. I created careers for them. If you were to take a stand for me running the business, I am sure everyone would step up to the plate. After all, it is half my business too.

And we created it together as a way for us to take care of our children's future. I think it is solid enough now that if you don't want to be the main teacher, you won't have to be. That was always our plan. Plus, the leadership and horses' classes I bring to the business produce good revenue," Emma offered.

"No. I don't want you to run the business anymore. I want you to focus on making more money with your horse business."

"Hmm." Emma didn't know how to respond. His words, "I'm done with parts of the marriage," rang in circles in her head. *How can you be done with parts of a marriage? Is that like the pelican is done with one of her wings? How does our marriage survive with one wing?*

Emma had a dream that night that she was on board the Titanic. She was at the rail, looking down at her children, waving goodbye from the dock below. She was smiling and waving back at them as if everything was okay. And yet she knew, or perhaps more accurately, her spirit knew, that this was a most dangerous quest into the icy waters before her.

When Emma awoke the next morning, she didn't want to admit how alone she felt. Here she was on vacation with her family, and she felt guilty that she was not grateful enough. Could that be why her husband seemed so angry and distant? She had always thought of herself as brave and strong, able to withstand hardship and pain. Look at how much Smiley—and the pelican—had been able to take.

She loved her husband, her kids, and her home. But she still wasn't ready to see that she was losing ground in saving her marriage. She thought she could out-will her feelings of betrayal and exclusion. She believed that if she loved enough, everything would be okay—and her love would be returned.

But that was not her experience now. No matter how hard she tried, she could not figure out why her husband was shunning her. The vacation was not bringing them closer together. She could barely feign a smile for her kids to pretend she was having a good time. She wanted to play with them in the water, but she was afraid they would feel her deep sadness, and she didn't want them to experience the pain she was in. She put her spirit self in the stall to suffer alone and in silence. That is all she could do.

Her logical mind took charge. "Emma, if you can figure out what you're doing wrong, you'll be able to fix things," it told her. Her logical mind wouldn't admit that something was desperately wrong and she was not to blame. She continued to deny the quiet storm that had taken hold inside of her heart. As her pain grew into a small flame, the tears of her idealism squelched the fire.

The metaphor of the Titanic was like her own silent movie relentlessly playing over and over. Not the romantic part, but the women in their finest attire boarding a sinking ship. Everyone said the Titanic was unsinkable. They had no doubt. In fact, they didn't even put enough lifeboats on the ship because they were so sure that nothing would go wrong. The engineers and financiers logically determined Titanic's stability and strength were like no other ship. It simply would not sink.

Emma remembered Liam's first question on the beach when they saw the cruise ships docked offshore. Was his obsession with lifeboats actually his intuition, feeling that her perfect metaphoric ship—her marriage—was doomed to sink and she needed a lifeboat that wasn't there?

Liam was intuitively linked to her from birth and she to him. At home, he built boats out of corks glued together and cardboard boxes stacked three stories high. Some had furniture in them like the Titanic. He always made sure they had lifeboats. It was too daunting for Emma to think about the significance further, and she distracted herself by finding shells in the sand and watching her son play at the water's edge.

She thought about the pelican. Its terrible fate is yet another example of Mother Nature's mercilessness. She is not sentimental. When it's time for her to sweep her harsh hand, she does so without pause.

"Am I too sentimental?" she pondered as if the sand would reply back to her. "Is the pelican a metaphor for me? Is it that obvious that I am dragging my broken wing, pretending everything is okay? I can't fly without both wings, and if I can't fly, I will die."

No one came to her rescue, not even her great-grandmother. A few tears fell before she sucked up her courage, gathered Liam in her arms, and headed back to the room where the rest of her family was waiting.

As a child, Emma only received her mother's love when she was sick or injured. She learned early in life to hide her wounds because she didn't want that kind of love. Maybe that had something to do with why she cared for wounded animals as if hoping for some healing in exchange.

Her father had taught her to turn the other cheek. Most of the time, this was a reasonable strategy. But sometimes the cost was too high. What about her ancestors who turned their cheeks, only to be slaughtered and put in concentration camps and on reservations?

To sacrifice her spirit for another's glory was a dangerous quest. To pretend the inequities of the world didn't exist was like getting on board the Titanic in a pretty dress and pearl necklace, filled with the illusion of reaching the other side of the sea in fashionable form.

Deep down inside, Emma's spirit tried to prepare for the icy waters of her impending fall. But her logical mind didn't listen, and she stayed aboard the doomed Titanic because that was the only thing she knew how to do.

It's Not Poetry

It's not poetry
To see a pelican dragging its broken wing down the beach
Past the sunbathing tourists staring at the majestic bird
Drinking their margaritas while turning the pages of their
novels.

It's not poetry
To imagine the lone pelican flying gracefully along her daily
route
So many feet above the ocean where the tourists romp
Only to have her wing sheared off by a passing parasail
As the humans under the parachute
Imagine what it would be like to fly.

It's not poetry
To look that pelican in the eye and have nothing to say
Except, "It's okay."

Even the poet is crippled without her bow and arrow
Incapable of assisting in another's suffering.

And the poet wonders why?
Why god? the poet asks.

And the pelican continues her walk down the beach,
Her wing dragging behind her.

Opportunities and Contemplations

REFLECTION

Witnessing the injured pelican and realizing that no one else noticed or cared was inconceivable to me. I felt like the pelican was me, sending me a visceral, visual message I could not deny. I couldn't stop thinking about the pelican. The hotel staff shot her that evening to put her out of her misery because they didn't want to make an effort to save her.

I didn't plan on using the Titanic as my metaphor. It was simply there, ready for me to notice it. But I did feel like I kept putting on a pretty dress and my pearls, hoping my broken wing would miraculously heal itself. In the same way, I hoped the birds that were not releasable at the Raptor Center of my youth would somehow be able to be healed. Otherwise, they would be euthanized. For without a wing, they were not useful unless they could be tamed to the fist. And the center only needed so many non-releasable birds to send a message to the youth.

It wasn't until I wrote this chapter that my logical mind finally listened to my spirit self and acknowledged and allowed my pain to come to the surface so I could begin to forgive myself and make sense of the slow demise of my marriage.

No one was listening to my SOS calls, not even me. The signs were in front of me: the ticking tarantula time bombs, the pelican and her broken wing, the Titanic with no lifeboats. I had never felt so alone with my family. I wanted to cry into my wine glass at the dinner table, dining on fine food. But I didn't. I wouldn't. I held my head high, just as I knew my grandmothers did. It ran in my blood that way.

The Titanic is rich in metaphor. It was an unsinkable ship, and yet it sank. Think about the juxtaposition of wealthy women (domesticated women) in pearls coming to America at a time when the land was being taken away from Native Americans by rape, pillage, massacre, slavery, and other extreme means.

What truths and lies are forbidden or hidden? Why do we humans allow so many untruths to be true? What does sanity mean? What does insanity mean?

WHAT SEEMED UNSINKABLE SANK

- Do you have a Titanic metaphor, "the unsinkable ship," that is relevant for you to explore?
- Do you have a different metaphor besides the Titanic? Go for it.
- What does the logical, rational side say?
- What does your intuition say?
- Do you need to take a stand for yourself, even if it means disappointing people?
- Who are you afraid to disappoint?
- Now write a story about another option, an alternative that does not end in capsizing.

TIME IN NATURE CONTEMPLATION

Find a quiet place to sit in nature. Bring your blanket and some tea. Make a place setting for your logical side and another for your intuitive, non-linear side. Let them each have a turn. Don't let one interrupt the other.

Later, reflect on:
- What is the quality or tone of each voice?
- Which side opens and which side closes?
- What conversations or stories do you want to change?

Helga

Not one storm, but many storms pelted the sheep fields once Emma got home from Mexico. Like a relentless lover, the rain poured without pause for days on end. The usual winter landscape had turned dark and wet like the belly of a whale. Each winter, Emma expected a serious storm like this, with torrential downpours and heavy winds, but not one after another. Already the kids had been out of school for three days because the roads were too flooded to travel.

She had learned from many winters in this coastal land that one could not predict when the storms would come to humble humanity or how significant they would be. There had been some winters when the valley did not receive enough rain, and the land and animals suffered in the ensuing summer months. And when the seasonal deluge did grace the land, however brutal, one never knew what months the storms would finally arrive.

What Emma did know is that heavy rain and horizontal winds for several days in a row was a serious matter for all: the young hawks unable to hunt, the old barn owls blown into the low-lying hills in the dark of night, the horses shivering with their heads down, soaked and losing weight with each breath. Emma worried especially about the young lambs being born in the cold, wet darkness. The mama ewes were not even able to lick the placenta off their newborns, hopelessly trying to dry off their quickly drowning babes.

I shall call this storm "Helga," Emma thought as she awoke early to check for newborn lambs. Emma's flock was still in the midst of lambing season when Helga, the dark hand of the storm, mercilessly chose to strike. Emma was angry with Helga and had pleaded with her for a break for a day or two, so the animals could recover from her beating.

Emma knew that Helga didn't care, that she was part of some larger scheme that no human could ever hope to control. Emma put on her mud boots and water-resistant coat, knowing it really didn't repel water.

"Why don't you wear waterproof pants, so you don't get so wet?" her logical mind asked. "I hate the plastic and its lifeless feeling," answered her spirit self, "not to mention its terrible toxicity to all life on earth." And the truth was, she liked, just a little, the wetness that reminded her how vulnerable she was, like the animals that she admired.

She took a deep breath and unbolted the door, which immediately blew open, pressing against her, rain attacking the floor. Head down, she pushed out into the storm. Emma checked the barn to make sure the roof had not blown off. Already this storm had leveled one neighbor's barn, the once majestic protector lying in crumpled humiliation. Her other neighbor had awakened the previous morning to find his 2,500-gallon water tank missing. It had blown across five fences and three property lines—a distance of more than two and a half miles—only to come to rest at the bottom of the lowest field it could find.

Water was rushing off the land, forming new paths that Emma had never seen before, rushing toward the bottom of the valley as fast as it could—as if it were in a race against time. The seasonal creeks burst beyond their borders, which failed at their usual attempts to control the flow in an orderly fashion as the water, driven by gravity, pummeled down. The estero at the bottom of the valley swelled beyond its own imagination as it tried desperately to move the water toward the ocean. The low-lying roads that meandered on either side of the estero were nowhere to be seen, forcing the human traveler to a halt.

So, while the land had no time to ponder, Helga had masterfully forced the local humans to a halt. As Emma headed down the steep driveway to the lower pasture, she noticed tourists with fanciful notions of seeing the beauty of the California coast stranded in their cars on the highway below. They had not respected the flood signs where the estero met the highway at the bottom of her driveway.

"Do they really think their cars can swim?" Emma mused. She decided to drive to the edge of the flooded road to see if she could help. As soon as she saw that the waters had gobbled up the fence line, she knew she would not make it through. She turned around where the flooded road disappeared before her as a BMW drove past her four-wheel-drive truck. She tried to wave them down and tell them not to enter the murky waters, but they didn't listen. The naïve travelers quickly discovered that water will enter a car. Helga didn't care about them and their shiny car. They were stranded in the middle of the flood, their car ruined from inside out. They were forced to wait for someone, *anyone*, to rescue them.

There was nothing she could do to help them, so Emma made her way back up the driveway. Looking out, she saw a downed lamb in the west field. Her heart paused, trying not to get her hopes up and, at the same time, trying to buckle up and prepare herself for the worst. She had already lost three lambs to Helga. She swiftly jumped out of her truck, opened the gate, and headed toward the lamb. As she approached, Emma was struck by the stark whiteness of the little body on the green landscape, like a white lily, so fresh and inviting.

Emma bent down and lifted the limp body out of the small puddle of water that covered the grass. The lamb was cold, wet, and barely breathing. Emma's only choice was to take the babe from its mom and try to save it. She wrapped it in a towel and tried to dry it off, even though the rain tried to undo her efforts. She tucked it into her coat, made her way back to the truck, and headed for the house. But by the time she got home, the babe had died. Emma put the lamb's nose up to her cheek to see if she could feel her breathing. She held her hand over the lamb's heart. It was silent.

"Dammit!" Emma exhaled.

Her head bent in sorrow, Emma held the limp babe to her chest, carried her outside, and laid her on the ground. She took a shovel and dug a shallow grave. She placed the lamb in her final resting place, still thinking that she could do something to save the lamb. Her body knew differently as it slowly placed the heavy soil over the white coat. The voices of her ancient ancestors spoke a prayer: "Go peacefully, young one. Come back in a new life, a stronger body, and a better time. Visit us again. You have a place here."

Emma went back out into the storm, even though she was sopping wet. The wind had let up a bit. She checked the flock again and noticed a ewe lying in an unusual position. As she came closer, the ewe did not get up as it normally would when approached. Beside her was a young lamb trying to keep warm. The ewe was old and thin, her ribcage heaving in long, slow breaths. Emma picked up her sunken body and assisted her to the shed to get her out of the rain.

Emma lay the ewe down on the damp earth and offered her food and water. The ewe was too weak to eat. Her lamb stood by watching but ran away as Emma tried in vain to catch her. After numerous attempts, Emma left. There was nothing else she could do for now.

The next day, as the storm began to fade, Emma visited the old ewe. She was weaker than the previous day. Emma knew the animal was near death. She continued to offer her food and water over the next few days, but the ewe refused. Emma could tell that the ewe was fighting for her life so she could care for her baby, but she saw defeat in the ewe's eyes.

Emma and the ewe looked at each other for what seemed like hours. Spontaneously and without thought, Emma softly spoke. "I promise you I will take care of your baby. I will keep her alive. You can let go now."

That afternoon, when Emma checked the ewe, her old body lay limp and still, already becoming the earth from which she had originally sprung. Emma remembered her vow to the ewe and tried to catch the lamb. The lamb was wild and full of fear. It took three more days for the lamb to finally succumb to Emma's attempts to save her, her fragile young body weak from hunger. Emma picked her up and felt the baby's warm body relax into her arms.

"I will take care of you, dear one. You are safe now." Little did Emma know how important this little "woman of wool" would become. Their destiny together had begun.

On the way home, Emma named her Elsie. It was important to have a name. It took two days for Elsie to accept a bottle. Emma had to pry her mouth open and beg her to nurse. She finally resorted to plunging a syringe of milk into her mouth to stimulate her appetite. It worked, and the lamb began to survive once again. Elsie started to relate to the six other bummer lambs—babes with no mothers—in her pen. She was different compared to the other orphaned lambs. She had a deep look in her eyes—as if she knew something the rest of them didn't know, as if she were contemplating the meaning of life and what it meant to have survived her mother.

Emma knew she couldn't speak of this to the other ranchers who were all men. They might think she was soft. Already, they didn't quite know what to make of a woman rancher. Sometimes she tried to be *just a woman*, but most of the time, she forgot. She'd find herself talking with the men around the barbeque at community gatherings instead of being inside cooking with the women. Her husband scolded her. He thought it was inappropriate for her to talk with the men about ranching adventures, even though she was a rancher.

Emma wondered if the men respected her. It seemed like they did. They often asked her about her sheep and horses. They included her in the local conversations about weather and how it affected the pastureland. But overall, it didn't matter to Emma if they respected her as a rancher or not. She had learned a long time ago that she was on her own, an outcast of the human world but stuck in a human body.

In some strange way, Elsie reminded her of this. The lamb was on her own, too, and she knew it. She and Emma formed a bond; they had a quiet understanding of each other. Unbeknownst to either of them, they needed each other at this time, in this place.

Over the next few days, Elsie gained strength and began to frolic with the other lambs. They were a bundle of cuteness, full of pink noses and soft eyes, eagerly awaiting life. Bellies full, they romped with joy. Life seemed good in the pale straw pen that was now their home. They had forgotten the storm that had orphaned them.

One morning, Emma stayed longer than usual in the pen. The early sun rays beamed through the open window of the barn as she sat down and let the babes smell her face with their warm muzzles, the smell of sweet milk still on their lips. Elsie came close as Emma grew quiet. Emma had the distinct impression that Elsie did not think of herself as a sheep.

"You seem to know why you are here," Emma spoke to the little one in silent words.

"Yes, I do." Elsie's eyes shined deep into Emma's heart.

"You are very sweet."

"I know," Elsie replied simply.

"Your mother was so brave. I promised her I would take care of you."

Elsie looked up again into Emma's eyes, blew on her cheek, and scampered off to the other lambs. After a few minutes, they piled up and fell asleep for a morning nap. Without further thought, Emma got to her feet and finished feeding the horses, chickens, and goats. It was peaceful among the animals and the quiet of the barn. Emma felt at home and in her place here.

One of Emma's favorite afternoon rituals was having a silent conversation with the mama barn owl. Every spring, she nested with her young in the owl box Emma had placed high up in the barn rafters. When the little owls got old enough, they roosted on the highest eaves inside the barn. They rested silently by day, blending into the woodwork so no one could see them.

It didn't matter to Emma if it were words or images that carried their silent thoughts back and forth. She had long ago let go of needing to know in human terms why she could speak to animals and they to her. She had spent too many years with them to need an explanation.

On the other hand, some of her students and colleagues, peers, and competitors needed to "understand." They wanted to know *how* to talk to animals. They wanted proof that it could be done. They reminded Emma of her days in college when her professors insisted that animals don't have feelings or experience emotions. She knew they did.

Emma was busy getting the barn ready for her upcoming equine-guided coaching class. Fourteen attendees were on their way to her ranch, traveling from around the world. They wanted to learn about horse communication, but Emma knew they would learn much more about the silent conversations of plants, animals, and even their own spirit selves. They would learn the essence of what it feels like to be interconnected with nature.

For the first few weeks, the students struggled with their own internal truths and lies. The horses mirrored everything the students felt. They mirrored their self-judgments; they mirrored their inner spirit's desire to be free of the "shoulds" and the "shouldn'ts." They stomped their feet when someone was angry. They walked up to students and put their heads in their heart space when they were being honest. Every interaction was new and unique. It fascinated Emma how accurate the horses were.

In her teaching, Emma followed the way the horses reflected each person. She sorted out the clutter of self-judgments and harsh words (those old lies) and held the warm, lighted lantern out to show their weary minds that, if they let go of their old battles, their spirits could be free. Then they could realign with their destiny and be connected to the Great Spirit once again.

This class was particularly hard. The students, many of them accomplished coaches, resisted the depth of coaching that the time with the horses provided. They knew the horses saw into their insecurities, and they didn't like it. They wanted to look like they had it all together. Some of them wanted to gain Emma's skill, but they didn't want to do the hard work, their own self-work to clean out the interior clutter in the old closets of their minds. Their rational minds resisted being authentic because that might show weakness. They didn't see it was their own demons pelting them with self-judgment that created a level of incongruency the horses would not tolerate.

One night, as Emma came into the house weary and emotionally exhausted after twenty days of teaching and healing, Ken bluntly said, "You know, Emma, you are not a teacher. You are not a healer. I don't know why you are bothering to work so hard at it. Why don't you spend more time in your studio painting? Or what about running someone else's company? You are good at that."

She didn't even have time to put down her books. The words, "you are not a teacher," rattled through her brain like a ninja star, cutting and tearing away at her very sense of being. She felt nauseous like she was going to throw up. Emma was devastated.

"How can you say that? You know how hard it was for me to study with people. You know how hard I've worked. If you've always felt that way, why have you let me spend the last fifteen years of my career life helping you develop your programs?"

She had always admired and respected her husband's gift for teaching. She looked up to him, always asking him how she could improve as a teacher. How could he now say such a hurtful thing, especially after all of the hard work Emma had put into creating her own line of work to help people heal?

"You've been telling me to develop my own work. You don't want me to run our business anymore. I've been focusing on my work, yet now, once again, you seem angry at me, and I don't know why."

"We're not aligned." And with that, he turned away and walked down the hall.

Emma felt the powerful blow as if it had been a physical one. She reeled back and hit the red wall behind her, her legs wobbly from exhaustion. She picked herself up and went outside to weep. She didn't feel safe in her own house. She felt attacked when she was most vulnerable.

The dark night grew darker. The frogs on the pond croaked louder as she sunk into the watery underworld. Golda met her at the liquid bottom and whispered, "Now, do you see what I have been trying to tell you?"

The next morning, she woke up determined to work harder and try harder to prove her love and her worth. She taught for six weeks straight. First, a three-day leadership and horses program, followed by an international equine-guided education conference attended by over one hundred professionals, and then a five-week equine-guided training program. On the last day, as she led the fire ceremony celebrating her students' graduation, her husband shot his gun on the hill over the pond.

The gunfire ricocheted off the golden hills. The steely sound pierced the fire ring. Emma stood over the fire in disbelief, protecting the prayers of her students. "What could be more disrespectful?" she asked herself. "How can this be happening?" Even her students were alarmed. They, too, felt disrespected.

She thought about how angry her husband would have been had she ever done such a thing to him. She wondered why it seemed so easy for him to hurt her. Did her growing success and power threaten him? Emma didn't know the answers to these questions, but they burned inside her.

That night, trying to talk with him about it only led to a fight. Emma didn't want her children to witness the disrespect she felt in her marriage because she didn't want them to think it was okay. So, she took the high road. She stood tall and did her best to let it go, to turn the other cheek like her father always said.

Meanwhile, Liam played war on the floor. He brought the army men into the living room and set them up strategically across the Persian rug. As usual, he played both sides.

"Mom, which side is going to win?" he asked in all seriousness.

Emma was tired. She went for the easy answer and pointed to the side on the left. "That one."

"No, Mom!" Liam was irritated with her for not taking this more seriously. He wanted to understand the strategy. "Why will that side win? Why do you think that side will win?"

Emma didn't understand in the moment, but Liam was sorting out the internal battlefield he felt between his mother and his father. He was like a little horse, trying to show Emma that a war was at her feet. Emma was too tired to listen.

The days got longer. The people got harder. Their logical minds wanted to disqualify everything they were learning. If it were true that they made up their own lies, it meant that they were the only ones who could stop the lies and create new truths.

Some of them blamed Emma. "She's too harsh," they said. "She's too intense," they whispered among themselves after class. It was *her* fault they were uncomfortable. She could feel their judgments, and so could the horses.

Sometimes, the horses took one person out of the circle of humans as if to make clear who was creating the blame-and-shame trail beneath the surface. Those students didn't know that Emma had far more allies than they could see. The barn owls, ravens, and horses had her back.

At the end of each day, Emma went to her secret garden to slough off the human junk. Her animal and plant guides met her there.

"The human language is so inadequate in explaining animal communication," she complained late one afternoon as the air was getting cool and the sun was about to set. "It's so frustrating! Why are humans so difficult?"

Emma let her thoughts tumble out into the garden. "It's as if they're trying to rationalize, sort, quantify, separate, and categorize other people, animals, and plants to protect their sense of control," she said as she wandered. "After all, it must be someone else's fault—that's what they're thinking. They forget, don't want to know, or can't see that everything and everyone is connected. They're betraying the very subject they are attempting to understand."

"Nature does not live in human language," she continued. "It lives in the mysterious, invisible jet streams of air and mist, fog and silence. It lives in the emotions of ions. It travels on invisible paths between and through time and space—present, past, and future."

A silent debate ensued between Emma's animal self and her human rationale, which kept interrupting.

"I'm sure there are many ancient people who understand that animals communicate with greater clarity than many humans," Emma replied, not trying to hide her irritation. "Why did their nativeness get sacrificed and made wrong to separate man from nature? Why do church and science separate us?"

Her spirit self replied. "Maybe it is the human's false sense of separation from nature so they can dominate, control, and manipulate pretty much whatever they want, be it another culture of people, plant, animal, lake, river? Even the word 'native' has been demonized to be a person who is barely even a human being because they live so simply and close to the earth. How stupid is that?"

"Emma," her rational voice said. "Can't you accept the contradiction that you live in the world of humans? After all, you were born into the world as a two-legged."

"Why are you being so contrary, mind of mine?" she asked. "Whose side are you on anyway?"

She did not like being referred to as a human or two-legged. Emma felt her heels dig into the dirt. And with that, a hummingbird settled on a tree branch a few feet above her head and began to sing a twirly love song.

For the first time, Emma couldn't help but laugh at her own internal storm and the fight between logic and feeling, sense and sensibility. She thanked the bird of love and laughed again until happy tears lined her tired face. She picked some kale for dinner and went into her domestic abode for yet another dutiful night.

I Walk the Land Often

I walk the land often,
I ask the hills a question
I sit on the earth, feeling the cool dirt heat my blood
I look for a feeling, a sensation,
Where do I find courage?
What does forgiveness mean?

To feel the wind is to feel life
The ocean reminds me of my freedom to dream,
The soil under my feet teaches me perseverance
The moon reminds me of the great mystery of life.

And when I lose myself
And I need a shoulder to cry on,
I go to the forest and let my guides find me.
I feel at home in this place of belonging.

The forest is optimistic in the dark of day
The forest finds my way so that I will not stray.

While the rug gets pulled from beneath my feet,
The forest stays tried and true
So that I may see another day.

And when the evening fog sets in
The forest reminds me to go within
And find the arrow that cuts through the sky
That answers the question "why."

A day will come when all will be well and good
Even as the wind beats to and fro
Upon my fragile windowpane
Reminding my heart to beat again.

Opportunities and Contemplations

REFLECTION

The extremes of weather are Mother Earth's reminder of our permeability, mortality, and our lack of control. The storm shatters our ego, announcing that we are of little consequence in the bigger order of things. Our sentimental attachments are not significant. Helga is harsh, and she is real. At the time of this story, I was literally in the floodwaters of my pending fall. Metaphorically, my house was flooding and being swept off its foundation. I even had a dream the dam broke, and the water from the lake by our house tore through the foundation of our home. But I was not ready to see the metaphors around me calling for my attention.

In hindsight, all these years later, I can now see that there were so many alarm bells ringing: the fire ceremony, the little fire that makes the bullet fly into the hill with its harsh call, the fire burning in my heart, Liam's battle cries and fascination with whose side would win. And this part, Liam's need to figure out who would win. I wonder if it was some old battlefield of his past life, or his sentient knowing in this life, his sensitivity to the discord between his mother and father. The latter seemed more tragic than blaming it on some past blood memory.

I felt my husband pushing me away and replacing me with new muses—his other women students, particularly Prudence. I was knee-deep, or should I say hip-deep, in raising the kids and running the business. I begged him to talk about what was not working. "What do you mean we are not aligned?" I'd ask over and over again, only to watch him walk away down the narrow hall, leaving me alone. After all of my dedication to him, I didn't understand what he meant or was trying to say. There was a big fat lie between us, and the more I tried to find it, the further away it got. I tried being calm and centered. I tried being angry and upset. Nothing worked.

For so many years, I chose not to attend to my own pain. The cost was way too high to consider. First and foremost, I had to take care of my children. At the time, I felt if I took a stand for myself, it would cost me my marriage. I didn't want to do that to the children. I didn't want to hurt my family. My family is all I ever wanted. I banished the thought of divorce from my mind.

Instead, I tried harder to heal and rescue those in greater need than myself. But the world of people kept getting harder. There were people who believed me and wanted to walk with me, and there were those ready to make me wrong.

After I wrote this, I felt bad for my son, whose spirit self was trying to sort out the tension between his father and me. Now I can say I am sorry; I can listen with new ears. I can be more curious about how this time impacted not only me but my children as well.

THE STORM, PSYCHIC WARFARE, AND VULNERABILITY

- Journal about the metaphor of the storm, the shifter of shapes. What is the storm's nature, her or his character, personality? What is the lesson, the reminder for you and your environment?
- What does the storm want to wash away? Can you let it? It is your time to wash clean of the past.
- Do you ever feel split between two different realities or worlds? Does it ever feel like a battlefield? What side is your side? What is the other side? Who is being impacted by the dis-order?
- Is your inner mind conflicted? Do you hear yourself warring between your rational mind and your intuitive knowing?

- Create a dialogue between the different parts of yourself. How do you make sense of your dual, or even multiple, realities?
- What are new choices and interpretations you can shapeshift into?

TIME IN NATURE CONTEMPLATION

Find a place you can go where you can be around animals—a dog park, a horse stable, a zoo, a pet store, the forest, or an aquarium.

Have a silent conversation with the animals. Do the conversations come in the form of a story, an image, or a dialogue?

What are the silent conversations, and how do they travel?

Explore the questions, not with the purpose of answering them, but allowing them to become channels for a silent transfer of information.

Elsie's Courage

The cool April winds delivered their usual coastal flare—blunt and direct. Emma liked coastal winds. In the same way people from Alaska knew snow, Emma knew wind. She knew the difference between a spring wind and a fall wind, with its dry, earthquake-like hum. A winter wind usually came with horizontal rain, like an angry mother sending you to your room for the night. Mid-February winds teased you, bringing warm smells, enticing you to imagine that summer had arrived. The two-leggeds would don their shorts and tank tops, only to find turtleneck rains the next day.

Spring winds from the coast were strong and made the hillside grasses dance toward the horizon. Sometimes it would be too windy to ride, too unpleasant to take a walk, and plain irritating.

Fall winds brought fires. Emma could sometimes smell a wind foretelling of burnt embers. She liked the smell of an evening campfire, but the smell of fire reminded her of another time. When she was five years old, her mother had sternly taken her arm and said, "Come with me."

Emma was scared by her mother's aggressiveness. Her mother sat Emma down on the kitchen floor, took some cloth from one of Emma's dresses, put it in the pie pan, and lit it on fire.

"Do you see how easy fabric burns?" she insisted with an angry tone as if Emma had done something wrong.

Emma was frightened, so she agreed, "Yeah."

"Never play with matches! You could light yourself on fire," her mother said. And then she wept.

Emma sat quietly while her mother buried her face in her hands. She was too young to understand why her mother was crying, but she knew it was of great importance. It wasn't until years later that Emma learned that her cousin, not much older than she, had lit her dress on fire with her mother's matches while the mother lay drunk on the floor. Her five brothers and sisters ran into the house, hearing the child's screams, but they could not save her.

It still made Emma cry to think of the little girl in her flowery dress, torched by her own innocence. To this day, whenever the campfire burns or a good winter fire crackles, Emma becomes mesmerized by the way the fire dances, so beautiful and yet so dangerous. She sees death and rebirth in the embers.

Of course, she passed down to her children the importance of not lighting yourself on fire. Her son, Liam, was in love with fire like she was. But he was not afraid of it. He had earned a reputation for burning things: pillows, bugs, batteries. He masterminded a paper boat that could float in the pond outside their house, rigged with a device that would catch the boat on fire. He even placed roly-polies, those bugs that roll up into little balls, on the boat, complete with mini-lifeboats, so he could count how many survived.

Why had this fiery memory come to her now? She didn't know. It was April, after all, the grasses still moist and green, and there was no sign of fire on the wind that day.

Elsie was healthy and old enough to return to the flock along with the other bummer lambs. Her coat was pearly white. Emma and her son carried the woolly lot of lambs to the back of the pickup truck one by one and drove them down the hill to the pasture below. Emma had fulfilled her promise to the old ewe. At least, she thought she had.

The pleasure of setting the little lambs free made up for much of the winter's plight. With smiles on their faces, mother and son walked the perimeter and shyly looked on as the older ewes approached the babes and nuzzled them into the circle. The field was a brilliant fluorescent green. The sun was shining bright on the field as if trying to dry up the wetness of the last storm. As she listened to the little bubbles of water trickling to the surface and the mud sighing, Emma was reminded of how much she loved to listen to the land speak.

Days later, Emma felt a need to go down to the lower field. She didn't even stop to think of why she wanted to go; she just went. On her way, she had a thought about cleaning up the old hay shed, even though she knew she had more important things to do.

As she nonchalantly opened the old door, a noise in the dark corner of the shed startled her. Everything was in disarray. Sheep poop was strewn beside her boots, and an old cupboard lay toppled on the ground. Something wasn't right. The cupboard was jiggling, almost like it was dancing to music. Emma picked it up, only to find Elsie lying in an awkward pile. She was wet from her own urine and thin as a board. How Elsie had gotten into the old shed was beyond comprehension. Nonetheless, there she was: near death with a broken leg.

"Oh Elsie, what am I to do with you? How on earth did you get into this mess?" Emma picked up the limp lamb and took her to the big barn by the main house.

"Most ranchers shoot sheep with broken legs," Emma said to the babe as she dressed her leg. "Did you know that? Now, this is your second near-death experience. First, you lost your mom, and you wouldn't let me catch you. You almost starved to death. So, I'll make you a deal. We will give your spirit a fighting chance, but you've got to stay with me. You got that?" Emma lovingly hugged Elsie.

To stabilize the broken bone, she wrapped the lamb's broken leg with a few flat tongue depressors, cotton, and vet wrap. Over the next several days, she tended to the lamb with ardent care. Everything seemed fine until, one morning, Emma found Elsie in the back of her little handmade woodshed, nose to the ground. She made a gargled sound with each breath of air.

"Dammit, Elsie, what's the deal here? Are you on a death mission? You have to stay with me." Emma was both irritated and concerned. The lamb had pneumonia. It was hard to say how she got it, but Emma felt a moment of defeat wash over her.

And then, as was Emma's nature, when the thought of giving up gained momentum, her tenacity for life grew tall. She filled a syringe with penicillin, knowing that if she gave Elsie the shot, she would have only a fifty-fifty chance at living. Half the time the sheep would die from the antibiotic.

Emma spoke silently to Elise. "Well, we don't have much to lose. If I don't give this to you, you will die. What do you think, Elsie?"

Emma gave a small prayer before she plunged the syringe into the sick lamb's muscle. "It would be a shame for you to go so soon, young one. I can see you being strong and free. I see you fulfilling your destiny as a mother. And besides, I made a promise to your mother."

Elsie squirmed at the sting of the shot. Emma left some food and water and went about her chores, trying not to feel her concern or the mercilessness of life.

The next day, Emma was shocked to hear Elsie calling, "Baaa, Baaa," as she reached the barn to do the morning feed. She sounded hungrier than ever. As Emma made her way down the breezeway, she could see the lamb waiting for her, standing on all four legs.

"Wow, it worked," she cried. "We did it! Good job, Elsie."

Love

Love doesn't mean "turn the other cheek"
While the devil is at your feet.
Love doesn't mean not feeling the pain
Pretending it'll be alright again.

Love has nothing to do with right and wrong
Love has only to do with what you hold strong
Your ideals, your beliefs
Even your shadows and griefs.

Love makes you feel!
Oh, yes it does,
It is so real.
Sometimes it feels too much
Because you can't use it as a crutch
To shy away from all that's so.
It is the first thing to go
When afraid or hurt,
The first thing buried in the dirt.

To bury your heart
To avoid the pain
Is too high a price to pay.
It's not good enough to shy away.

For without a heart
Think of all the good that's lost
Like hell in its eternal frost,
Too cold to bring new life,
There is no beauty without strife.

Don't you see
That when you love, all are free,
Like the hummingbird and the honeybee,
Or the white dove high in the highest tree.

With love, you choose
To touch those whose
Hearts grew cold long ago, and full of fright.

With love, you know,
It grows beyond a smile
and warms someone's cold night for a while.

With love, you know,
You fill the air with hope,
Even tired lungs that grope.

Love means that in spite of it all,
You'll not fall prey to unfairness,
but instead, stand tall.

With love, you know,
Even though you witness mass injustice in every alley,
On every street,
You'll not forget to stay on your feet.
Feel your heartbeat,
Your drum, your call.
Do not forget it all.

Do not let your heart close.
Do not die before the rose.
Do not forget to feel your life
Even when it is full of strife.

Love is all the colors in the rainbow
Only time will show,
Dark can become light
And we can live without fright.

Opportunities and Contemplations

REFLECTION

Nature has always come to my aid in so many ways, sending me signs, inspirations, and hope. The key is to be present and listen. Elsie reminded me of how I listen, reconnect to my life source, and how important nature is to me. She reminded me of love and commitment. She reminded me of motherhood.

Elsie was another mirror of me. She had a will to live, yet her mother was not able to defend her and protect her. Today, I can see myself in this tenacious lamb, and this inspires me.

There was a tension between the not-yet-felt power to heal myself and the powerlessness I felt at this time in my life. My intuition was listening to Elsie. I didn't yet know that my opportunity was to become my own best parent. I could learn to have the same determination for my own survival and health as I so easily gave to Elsie.

Every geographic terrain has its unique weather patterns and extremes. For me, the weather is a major character in my life. It brings to me the quality of energy I am supposed to be present to. I am curious about what its lesson is, or perhaps better said, what it is asking me to remember or accept. What does it allow or disallow? What kind of attention or emotion is it asking of me?

HOW DO YOU TAP INTO YOUR INTUITION?

- Who in your life gives you inspiration and hope?
- How do you empower yourself?
- How do you empower others? Is there a discrepancy?
- Is it time to become your own parent?

TIME IN NATURE CONTEMPLATION

On your walk or meditation in nature, reflect on the Great Mother's presence and purpose. Ask her what being sentimental means. Ask her about being fair. Why does she do what she does? What would you like to say to her? Would you like to ask something of her?

Finding Emma

The divide between Emma's efforts to provide a healing place for people and her efforts to mend her broken marriage grew and grew. Ken didn't like her friends or students. When he was out of town on business, she felt comfortable inviting her friends over. But when they saw his headlights come up the long hill toward the main house, they said a quick goodbye, jumped in their cars, and headed off.

Emma and the kids were in their own little groove while he was away. When Ken returned from a work trip, Emma's relationship with the kids would change—even their home environment was affected. Emma made sure the house was neat and clean when he got home because she knew he had a habit of throwing their things away if they were left out. Each week, when it was time for her to take the trash to the bottom of the road, she sorted through the trash and rescued the items that were meaningful to her or the children, including her personal possessions and the kids' toys.

On one occasion, Emma discovered Ken even threw away a set of her ancestors' sterling silver salt and pepper shakers that had been in her office, which made Emma feel that the things she cared about and her personal space were not respected.. She had asked him not to throw away her or the children's belongings. She tried to explain that the kids' games were useless if they were missing pieces. Her requests fell on deaf ears.

On another occasion, when Ken returned home late from a two-week business trip, he took the colorful vases Emma had placed on the kitchen window sill and put them in the darkest corner of a cupboard as if to say, "No flower power here. This is *my* kitchen. It's mine. You have no power here."

While it bothered Emma immensely to walk into the kitchen the next morning and find her things missing, she simply took the vases out of the dark dungeon and refilled them with flowers.

She planted a bigger garden, put on a prettier face, and tried harder to make her marriage work. But it wasn't working. Ken grew angrier and more hostile. Emma started to notice that when he was home, Liam would make a joke at her expense, and the whole family would laugh and roll their eyes at her, just like Ken did. It was supposed to be joking, but it wasn't funny to Emma.

One night after dinner, Ken walked away from her while she was speaking, yelling down the hall behind him, "We're done."

"What do you mean we're done?" Emma pleaded as she followed.

"We're not aligned," he said and waved her off.

"What do you mean?"

Her mother's haunting words, "You don't love me," joined the party.

Feeling desperate, she queried silently: *What does this mean? What does this mean? These are not truths; these are lies. How can you say such things? Why are you walking away from me? I don't understand.*

Emma wanted to return to the safety of the animal world. She was ready to be invisible again. But the voice of her great-grandmother, the one she had never known in this life but knew in her deepest being, called to her in a seductive voice that Emma could not refuse: "No Emma, it's too easy for you to turn back. You can always come home. You know this. Your destiny is to walk a path that others can follow."

"Yes, but what does the path look like?"

The old woman's face beamed. "You know it in your bones. It has no words."

"I know, I know. But what if I don't want to? It's too hard."

The next day, Emma's routine continued. After she got the kids to school, she went to the barn to work with a new client. Melissa had worked with her before and called with an urgent request to come and see Emma. Of course, Emma said yes.

Melissa was a high-level figure in a youth organization. She was loyal. She was a great worker. Her word was golden. Melissa lived and worked in one of the most violent cities in America. A tragedy happened when she witnessed a murder. She was working outside the building with a crew of contractors one morning when she heard a gunshot. She saw a teenage boy crash to the ground while the killer looked at her and ran off. She was the only white person and the only woman on the job. She ran over to the fallen youth who was in the throes of death. His eyes rolled into the back of his head; his hands and feet contorted in an unnatural position as he lay dying.

Melissa realized that the most humane thing to do was be with him as he passed. She sat quietly with him. Within a few minutes, the police arrived, pulled her away from the victim, and walked her a short distance from where the boy was lying. No one went to take care of the youth. He lay there dying alone. Her spirit was screaming, "Can't I be with him until the medics arrive? Someone needs to be with him!" No one listened.

Ten minutes later, the medics arrived, and the boy died alone. An hour later, she drove to her next meeting of the day, tending to business as usual. Melissa never registered what had happened. No one in her organization thought to offer her a few days—or even a few hours—off. She didn't consider it either.

Over the next few months, Melissa noticed more shootings in the city and heard sirens every half an hour. A fifteen-year-old high school girl was raped by ten men in front of twenty strangers, across the street from where she worked. Nobody called the police—not one person. And she went back to work.

Melissa started acting strangely, but she didn't realize it. She started cutting corners at work. She loyally attended all her meetings, but she had no emotion. She had deadlines to complete. But then her spirit quit. All of a sudden, out of nowhere, she had to go. She had the presence of mind to take a leave of absence. She phoned Emma. "I don't know what is happening to me," she said. "Can I come to the ranch and stay for a few days?"

"Of course," Emma said. "We'll see you soon." And she quickly got to work preparing a cabin for her.

Having the horses, the silent air, and the quiet breeze around was enough to allow the wounded woman's emotions to unfold. Each day, Melissa began to feel herself come a little closer to home. She told Emma and the horses what she had witnessed. She planted flowers around the cabins and helped around the ranch. After three weeks, she was able to go home and re-evaluate her work situation.

Emma's sense of reality was getting harder and harder to hold onto. Emma thought about the wounded woman who had come to the ranch for healing. Her experience hit Emma to the core as if she, too, had witnessed the murder.

She knew it was her turn to go inward; it was time to re-find her spirit. She placed a "closed" sign at the foot of her ranch. It wasn't visible to the outside eye, but Emma knew it was there. And so, she went quietly within.

The Duck Quacks

The storm has passed.
The silent darkness swirls around me.

The duck quacks noisily
Piercing the silence
Her call wrestles with the pond's dark surface.
She quacks
on an on
Announcing things to come.

I am trying to think, but her choir is all around me.
Now every insect and frog in my imagination joins in.

I am in the middle of nowhere.
How can it be so noisy in nowhere land?
I thought nowhere was dark and cold.

But the choir of life is so loud.
In the darkness, I see a doorway open
With a hint of something new.

It is the darkness before dawn.
The duck quacks noisily on the pond.

She says it's time to take action.
Enough thinking
It's time to trust your knowing.

It's time for your new life to begin.
Make no excuses
Don't wait for consensus.

Be bold.
Inspire yourself to take wing
And with that, she flies off the pond.

Opportunities and Contemplations

REFLECTION

As my crisis approached and my compassion grew weary, the only place I felt quiet was during my time in nature—walking the hills, sitting in the grass, looking at the pond, watching the birds, listening to the frogs. I was not giving myself the same respect I was giving others. My spirit was exhausted. And yet, my mind wanted to control my experience. I was still not ready to face my dilemma.

In my art studio, I painted horses in robes and a raven chief proudly wearing a robe and warrior headdress. I don't know why I was so into the metaphor of the robe. It seemed to be a symbol of power and protection. I didn't think much about it, really. I kept drawing and painting myself, horses, and ravens in robes.

One day, I had a vision of myself in my warrioress robe, running through the dark night. I was running for my life, bareback on a swiftly moving horse. We were tearing through brush and branches. We couldn't see where we were going as we clung to each other. My hands twisted in his dark mane, egging him on to go faster and faster. My spirit was calling me, holding out a light at the end of the forest. I felt a power rise inside of me. I was finally listening to my spirit call for help.

ARE YOU LISTENING TO YOUR SPIRIT'S CALL?

- Take out a blank page and let your spirit wander. Let your spirit express in words or images. What colors want to be chosen?
- What in your life no longer serves you? It could be a story about you. It could be the way a person treats you, a person with whom you need to change your relationship. It could be an attitude you have about what is possible or not for you.
- Is there something you witnessed that you want to release? It is not yours to hold onto. Put it on the page and let it go.

TIME IN NATURE CONTEMPLATION

Take time in nature to let yourself disappear into your imagination. Be the curious explorer. Who meets you there? What does freedom of spirit mean to the tree? What does it mean to you? Wonder, wander, be curious. What catches your attention?

Notice how you feel different in nature, if you do. What changes in your breathing? What changes in your senses? What does the air feel like on your skin? Notice your breathing. Write or draw a few words without planning, letting out whatever is there, no mind, simply being.

The Demon in the Gully

The day Chip arrived was cold and windy. The humans were bundled in their down jackets, hats, and mittens. The white trailer squeaked and churned as Chip wriggled around, trying to view his new surroundings.

Nancy, Chip's woman, daintily stepped out of the truck and immediately went to the trailer window to reassure Chip with soft words.

Emma took her mitten off and extended her hand to Nancy in the familiar human greeting. "It's nice to meet you," she said.

"Yes, it's nice to meet you too," Nancy said. "I have heard so many wonderful things about your place. I am so happy that Chip can come here and be a horse again. He's a rescue. He's a bit thin, and I have not been riding him since I got him."

"He will surely get to be a horse here," Emma said. "He will go out in the big field with the herd. But first, we'll put him in the corral next to the field for a few days so he can get used to the herd and they to him. Also, it is awfully hard to put weight back on a horse in the winter. You will need

213

to grain him every day to keep on the weight he does have."

She wanted Nancy to understand that caring for a horse in a fifty-acre field was a whole different process than keeping him in a stall. Emma had grown up around horses who could be horses on the land as they were meant to be. It was natural for her to let a horse's winter coat grow long and rugged.

But she had learned over the years that many new horse owners did not know how to let a horse be a horse. They wanted to blanket the horse, provide it with shelter, and feed it cookies and treats. Many stables kept lights on the stalled horses at night so their winter coats would not grow naturally long. *Why?* Because the horse owners didn't like wooly horses. They sweat sooner, and they're not as pretty.

Emma offered something different than most stables. She kept her horses in large fields and allowed them to form herds and attachments to each other. Emma remembered more than once when potential boarders had been too afraid to pasture their horse in the field because they wouldn't be able to catch it or the field was too windy for the horse. One lady decided not to board her horses with Emma because the driveway was too steep, and she would not be able to drive her trailer up and down it.

Another new horse owner who had lasted at Emma's ranch for only two months worried incessantly that her horse had ulcers. She wanted him in an outside pen so he could be *free,* but she worried about the footing of his pen getting wet. She also worried that his hay might touch the ground and he might get sand in his mouth. She had the vet out so many times Emma decided to ask her to leave before the energy of her worries actually *did* create an ulcer in the young horse's belly. Another gal had given her horse so many supplements that the poor horse's leg swelled to three times its circumference due to an overdose of salt.

"The grass is green now," Emma explained, "but it doesn't have a lot of nutritional value. We will want to get Chip in the field before the grass gets too rich, so he has time to get used to it. It'll come in around mid-February, and then we'll hope to see Chip gain weight. Until then, our best hope is to maintain the weight he already has."

Emma continued to educate her new client. "In May, the horses will often get ticks, and later, chiggers and no-see-ums. No-see-ums are like little mosquitoes that bite. The horses get super itchy. These are some of the things to prepare yourself for. Are you okay with that?"

"Yes," Nancy said. "I am so happy that Chip can live in an open environment. His mind was fried by his last owner, who put too much pressure on him as a jumping horse. My hope is that he will regain his confidence, settle down, and not be so high-strung."

As Chip backed out of the trailer, his dark bay coat hidden in his blanket, he took on a regal stance as if he were stepping toward his next winning race. Emma could tell that he was well-traveled. He had been a racehorse as a colt, and although he had never won much, he had tasted the roar of hoofbeats, the flared nostrils, and the stretch of sheer determination. Now, he smelled the other horses and let out a shrill whinny that was met by a cacophony of calls welcoming him to his new home.

As Nancy led him up to the stable, Chip pranced and bounced, snorted and bayed. Once in his new home, Nancy fussed over him as long as she could, and as the day grew to dusk, she got in her truck and headed home. Emma let out a sigh of relief; the barn was quiet again. She went over to Chip's pen and wondered why Nancy worried about him. Perhaps it was because he was her first horse and a rescue at that.

"You seem much quieter than most thoroughbreds off the track. Is your human the nervous type?" she asked Chip. He flipped his muzzle in an agreeing nod.

"Time will tell. Maybe you like to be slim like the running athlete that you are. I think you look fine, handsome even."

Chip's entry into Emma's herd was a laboratory of richness for anyone who noticed the subtlest of details. Emma loved to observe the herd dynamics change whenever a new horse was added. She could spend a lifetime in curious fascination, knowing deep inside that there was always something new to learn about the complexity and importance of this social instinct—a mirror reflection of humans.

She remembered Nancy asking, "When will you put him in the field?"

"When it seems right," Emma had offered. "Not before feeding time for sure. I'll wait until the herd is grazing peacefully and seems settled in their own relations together. I'll wait for a quiet day so that the energy of the transition is as smooth as possible."

Nancy wanted reassurance. "Will he be okay?"

"Most of the time horses are okay when integrated into a new herd, but you never know. Usually, there is a lot of hustle and bustle the first ten minutes, and then everyone settles down. It's when the new horse gets nervous and runs away from the herd that things get more intense."

Emma was glad she was the only one present the morning she finally let Chip go free with the herd. It was quite scary for people to witness the kicking, biting, squealing, and whirling about as the horses negotiated "who is who" in relation to each other.

Lacey, the lead mare, ran him down the field, teeth bared, followed by Superman, who ran faster and bit his rump. Chip bucked and took the bite but was not afraid. He kept coming back to the herd as if to say, "I want to be part of you." After a few minutes, the herd decided that Chip wasn't a threat to their established order, and he could hang out near them. Not *with* them, mind you, but *near* them. Chip was happy enough to graze on the outskirts.

Over the next two months, Chip continued to hang out at the edge of the herd. They still did not see him as one of them. Perhaps it was because he was so much bigger, being a thoroughbred. *Do thoroughbreds smell different than quarter horses?* Emma wondered.

She had learned that wild horses would not breed with horses who were so different in bloodlines, and it made sense to her. It explained why some horses never seem to integrate into certain domestic herds. Horses have a genetic memory and the ability to sense genealogy. This concept might seem like blasphemy to some, but to Emma, it was no different than the numerous bird species that scientists were finally recognizing had a genetic memory of their migratory path.

Even though he was not part of the herd, Chip had become extremely aggressive at feeding time. He would chase the lead mare and resident gelding off the hay. Emma was curious about this because no other horse had been able to do this before.

As she watched one morning, she noticed that Chip could move the other horses off the food, but when it came time to go out into the field, no one followed him or even included him. He would stay at the barn while the rest of the herd followed the narrow cut trail over the gully, down into the ravine, and up the steep hill to a sweet plateau of grass overlooking the barn.

Most people would assume that Chip had become the dominant gelding of the herd since he could push the other horses off the feed. But Emma knew otherwise. The lead horse, Lacey, set the pace and tone of the herd. Her place, as the direction-setter and decision-maker, was still intact.

Superman's position as the lead male, whose job was to keep the herd together when running from danger, was unaffected by Chip's presence.

Indeed, the herd seemed to dismiss Chip once their bellies were full. Sure, he was a bully on the surface, but the other horses didn't respect him. They easily left him behind each day.

Over the next few weeks, Chip began to follow them. But as he reached the gully, he paused. Emma could see that he wanted to go to the lush field with the others, but something bothered him about the gully. She didn't think much about it until Nancy came to visit Chip.

"I'm worried that he doesn't go over the gully," Nancy observed. "The field is so green on the other side. Doesn't he want to be with the others?"

"He does seem lonely once they've left, but something has him bugged about the gully," said Emma. "Someday, he will figure it out when the time is right for him."

Emma wasn't feeling well, so she headed up to the house to rest. This was unlike her; even her daughter noticed her withdrawn demeanor. She sat quietly, looking out the window as Nancy haltered Chip and set out toward the gully, encouraging the gelding to follow. She patiently walked over the cut in the path where the seasonal creek trickled downward on its determined path to the estero. Nancy tried for what seemed like hours to get Chip to cross the gully.

Emma watched, amused. "I wonder why it's such a big deal for Nancy that he gets over the demon lying hidden in the gully," she asked herself. "The gully's not even deep, nor is it that wide. A small hop would suffice."

But Chip did the same thing he did every day after morning hay: he walked up to the gully, stopped abruptly, backed away, and turned around.

Nancy persisted in trying to coax him. She even begged him with treats. Finally, after two hours, she walked up the hill to the house, knocked on the door, and asked Emma if she would help her get him over the gully.

Emma reluctantly agreed and walked down to the field. She tried several obvious methods of enticing him over the gully. After a half-hour, Emma stopped, paused, looked at Chip, and realized that if she really wanted to make him go over the gully, she could. But she simply did not need to prove her ability to force the horse into something that she did not have a big enough story about. She didn't care if he went over the gully or not.

For perhaps one of the first times in her life as a horse trainer, she told the unsweetened truth: "Nancy, you know, I could make him go over this gully. It wouldn't be pretty. But I am lacking a good reason to put him through a fight. There is something else going on here besides egos."

Emma was surprised with herself. This was so "un-trainer" like. And yet she really didn't care if Nancy understood her reasoning. She wasn't quite sure herself whether it was because she didn't feel well or if her psyche was renegotiating the traditional horsemanship model "you must make the horse do what you want when you want it." Emma felt into her belly; she didn't feel right about making him get over his demon if he wasn't ready. At least not today, and not in half an hour.

What does the gully remind Chip of? she wondered. *What memory does it spark?*

"Can you put his hay on the other side of the gully, so when he gets hungry enough, he might go over?" Nancy asked.

Emma looked at his slim frame and, despite her resistance, said, "Sure."

But that evening, she didn't have the heart to starve the horse in order to make him face his demon. She called Nancy the next day and explained that she had decided not to taunt him the way she had proposed. He needed to gain weight, and that seemed more important than Nancy's desire to make Chip do something he clearly had some reason for avoiding.

Life seemed to go back to normal around the barn. Each day, the herd left Chip at the gully as they headed for greener pastures. And each day, Chip stopped at the cut in the path and waited for their return.

Emma grew increasingly curious about Chip's battle with the gully. She thought of the numerous women who had attended her self-development programs and how each had some mysterious *gully* she was afraid to cross. For her students, the gully was symbolic of some deeper fear, a reminder of one's vulnerability.

The gully stood in the way of the tender reward of lush greens lying beyond the small leap of faith. Oh, but the *leap*! How grand it seemed—the gap between here and there, with the old self standing still, stuck in place, while the imagination grew rye and oat just out of reach.

What would it take for the fear to lose its hold—the fear of failing and falling into the bottomless pit where the fabled monsters dwelled? What act of courage would it take to step beyond the known terrain? What act of courage would it take to allow the body to follow its own imagination?

A few weeks later, Nancy called the vet out to the ranch to examine Chip. Emma wasn't sure why; perhaps Nancy wanted to see if he would be able to take a rider again. Emma quietly held him in the breezeway as the vet ran his hands down the horse's back. As he reached the place on the spine where the hip bones begin their articulation, his hands paused.

"You see this area here," the vet put his hand on the horse's rump. "Do you see how the left and right sides of his rump are not balanced? The right side is higher than the left. He has an old injury that prevents him from having normal flexibility. I see this often in jumping horses. You see, what happens is that the horse is heading over a jump, and as he gets to the other side, his front legs slip out from under him. He basically does the splits, tearing ligaments and tendons as he falls."

Emma finally understood why Chip wouldn't cross the gully. To get over the gully, Chip would have to reenact the motion that caused his injury. The thought of jumping over the gully brought back the memory of the pain and the humiliation of his past failure.

Finally, she could explain why it hadn't felt right to make him conquer his demon. He, indeed, had known better than they how he needed to protect himself. Emma had faith that Chip would overcome his fear when his body was ready—or when his desire to be with the others, to taste the sweet rye, outweighed his fear of falling. Either option was available to

Chip. Perhaps if Nancy stopped trying so hard to push him, to require he *get confident*, his imagination could flourish and overcome the demon of doubt.

"Light riding will be okay for this gent, but no jumping, Nancy," the seasoned healer instructed. And off he went to the next horse-human dilemma down the road.

A week later, as Emma was finishing a ride, she noticed the field horses heading for the upper pasture. For some unknown reason, she stopped what she was doing and watched as Sadie, one of the elder mares, hopped over the gully, followed by her son, Superman, and his son, Sunny. But what struck Emma on this warm morning was that Sadie turned around and looked back at Chip. The horses had not expressed care for Chip before now. It seemed like she was saying, "Come on. You can do it."

Chip looked at her longingly. His desire to follow her was palpable. To Emma's surprise, Sadie went back up to the gully, hopped over it, nuzzled Chip, turned, and hopped back. "C'mon," she whispered. She repeated this three times. Several other horses came back to Chip's side, paused, and then went over as if showing him that the gully was not so bad. He did not have to leap over it like a jump. He could step over it one foot at a time. Superman even stopped and stood right in the gully as if to imply that maybe it wasn't really a gully after all.

Sadie tried one last time, looked up the field, and began to leave. As she walked away from Chip, the light breeze brought the sweet smell of the fields, and before he could think, Chip lowered his head, sniffed the gully, and walked over it daintily, his hooves grounding him to the earth. The gully held his weight and, as he reached the other side, he let out a gleeful buck. The herd, all of them now, cheerfully set their tails to the wind and galloped up the hill.

Silly Mind

Listen you silly mind
with all your busyness
your righteous fervor
louder than a murmur.

Listen you silly mind
full of glorious fantasy
with your pompous way
as if you really know
as if I should believe what you say.

Silly mind
forcing my shallow breath
sending the flowers in my heart to death
but then, alas, I see
really, it's all about "silly me."

For why have I allowed you so much power?
Giving you my full attention, hour after hour.

Opportunities and Contemplations

REFLECTION

The gully reminded Chip of his old injury. Perhaps he had lost confidence in his abilities. Both his owner and I could see that the gully was no big deal. But the more Nancy pushed him, the more afraid he got. She wasn't listening to his fears. She wasn't curious about why he was so fearful. She was stuck in her plan, her agenda.

I intuitively felt it unwise to push him. I could have made him go over the gully, but my heart simply wasn't in it. I knew he had his reasons. It didn't feel right to force or dominate him to go over the gully to satisfy yet another human's agenda. I didn't have the energy left to abandon how I felt. I stood my ground and told Nancy I would not force him over the gully, nor would I starve him.

I've often wondered if it was in the subtlety of Nancy's accepting his fear of re-injury and no longer needing or wanting him to do the thing he was afraid of doing that allowed him to let go of the fear. Perhaps the release of her anxiety around the gully gave Chip permission to do the same.

It was then the horses waited for him and offered encouragement. In some way, their newfound patience to wait for him gave him the courage to follow them over the gully. And in so doing, he saw the gully wasn't as deep as he thought.

Chip reminds me of many of my clients. I wrote this story as an inspiration for them. It asks the question, "How do you overcome that perceived gully, that gap between your past life and your future life? And how do you approach that gully? Do you simply walk across it or jump over it?" At the same time, this story acknowledges that it is not easy. You must be ready; it has to be your time.

While I could see my clients struggling with their demons, I still couldn't see mine clearly. I was so busy taking care of everyone else and healing others I didn't see Chip's situation as a metaphor of my own. I even asked myself, "What is my gully that I am afraid to cross?"

I lied to myself, "I'm good. It's just a story about Chip and a good metaphor for those who are stuck."

In truth, I was terrified of my gully. If I turned toward my collapsing marriage, my whole world would fall apart. I couldn't see the other side of the gully. And I didn't feel like I had a herd of horses or friends waiting for me on the other side either.

More accurately, I didn't see the possibility of patience, acceptance, and support. I was consumed with the fear of failing, of not being good enough. I had lost the courage to fight for myself, to enforce my own free will. I had become the blamer and shamer of myself. I was whipping myself like Kerry whipped Smiley.

I've learned that sometimes you have to see someone with something else at stake before you can find the courage to take a stand for yourself. If you don't, others will also be hurt. For a rescuer like me, I could take the hits. I did that well.

Chip's entry into my life for the short time he was at my barn was life-changing. It was a stepping stone toward taking a stand with my clients as to how I would not treat their horses. I eventually asked Nancy to leave because she was such a nervous wreck, always worrying that Chip was going to get sick. I was afraid that *she* was going to make him sick. Perhaps intuitively, I knew I could not take her toxic energy anymore.

THE GULLY AS METAPHOR:
Is It Real Or Imagined?

- What gully lies between where you are now and where you want to go?
- What does the fear say would happen if you were to go over the gully? What if you jumped over it? What if you faced your fear?
- What new field could open up for you? Write or draw a picture of it. Give it some airtime.
- What is the "unsweetened truth" you need to tell?
- What's at stake in your life if you don't find the courage to take a stand?

TIME IN NATURE CONTEMPLATION

As you spend quiet time outside in nature, notice what your mood is. Be a keen observer. Begin noticing your mood before you go outside. How is your breathing? If you are tense, where are you tense?

Take some deep breaths and give your exhale to the wind, the air, letting it go so your lungs can fill with new air. Feel the oxygen feed your cells.

Look up into the sky. How do you feel?

Look at the ground. How do you feel?

Now, let your body's sensations wander. Journal about your sensations, how they change, how you shift from your busy mind to your somatic body.

Raven's Harsh Love

Every spring, the rafters of the barn were full of baby birds chirping. Most afternoons, Emma would find little baby birds who had fallen out of their nests. Some had died on their long trek to the hard soil, while others, naked without feathers, needed to be scooped up, placed in a warm box, and fed until they were ready to fly.

One breezy afternoon, Emma found a young female kestrel, the smallest of the falcons, feathered but not yet ready to fly. After she had carried the baby home, Emma looked into the box on the floor to see the little "she bird" looking up at her with innocence and peace. Little did Emma know at the time that the baby kestrel she had brought home that day foretold of immense changes in her life.

Emma had been calling in a magical, winged raptor, like the ones she had spent time healing in her youth. Her relationship with these birds was deep and wide, like the rich underworld at the bottom of the ocean. She had lived many years since holding them in her arms, healing them

227

with her touch. Now she was happy savoring their freedom all around, watching them circling above her or darting into the trees.

What could be a greater blessing? Somewhere deep inside, she had begun to feel a need to hold one close to her heart again, to look into its eyes like a mother looks into a child's eyes—or more profoundly, the way a child looks into the mother's eyes, with that deep understanding of each other's spirit. There is no judgment here, no humanness. And the mother knows, "Oh my god, this child of mine has seen no pain yet; she is full of possibility. Dare I allow any hint of what is to come, the pain of life to pass through my glance? Even if I answered, 'No, don't tell,' will I be able to pretend otherwise?"

The child's glance is still living in the multiple realities of existence. "How can I not honor that?" the mother says to herself because she knows it is true. And yet, her mother and father, grandfather, her whole town, city, and country have told her this is not so. But the universal archetype of the mother—the mother bear, mother wolf, mother horse—is all mothers that defend their children from the real world in those early transitions as the innocence of birth confronts the world as it is—blunt, careless, brutal, and unsentimentally real.

Emma knew this little girl falcon because it was simply her instinct to do so. She looked into her soft, knowing eyes, full of wisdom and tales of her fate, and she did not like what she saw. But the little bird didn't seem too concerned. She knew where she was going. Life to her was not just *this* life, in this new body. Freedom to her was her own ability to accept her destiny gracefully.

Despite what she saw, Emma whispered to the little one, "We are going to do *everything* to shape our destiny by inserting our free will here. If I am to care for you and ultimately set you free, you must meet me with all the determination, passion for life, and fight you can muster because there is a war upon us, dear."

Deep in her ancestral self, Emma knew what she had said to this small baby bird was true for her too. She knew it was up to her to save herself, but she was still hoping she could find a simpler way besides confronting her husband and possibly ending the marriage. She still felt betrayed by her husband and the employees of their business. They didn't take a stand for her and the value she had created in the organization they worked in. As a result, Emma went to the office less and less. It was too painful.

Her eyes fixed on the baby kestrel, Emma recalled the most recent chain of painful events. After dinner one night, Ken wanted to talk about his upcoming sixtieth birthday. He knew how much Emma loved to throw a party.

"I can't wait to plan a special celebration for your birthday. Do you have any special requests or desires for your party?" Emma asked inquisitively.

"Oh, Prudence, Jenna, and Nicki have already planned my birthday party," he announced proudly.

"Wow, that is a surprise! Why didn't you tell me this before?" she asked.

"They came to me and said they had it handled, that's all."

"Honestly, that is weird. I am your wife. That should be my job. Why didn't you tell them to talk with me?"

"It simply didn't occur to me. They seemed so eager," he replied without regard for Emma's feelings.

"Well, I want to be part of the preparation and celebration, so who shall I ask? Who is in charge of the plan?" Emma asked.

"You can talk to Jenna if you want to, but really, they have it all handled."

The next day Emma reached out to Jenna, and she confirmed that they didn't need or want her help. Emma denied that she felt embarrassed and ashamed for trying to insert herself into their plans, meeting resistance, and then giving up. She didn't know what else to do, so she sat back quietly and watched the other women plan her husband's party.

On the day of the event, she was given a seat at another table apart from Ken instead of being seated next to him at the head table. The other women had adorned the tables with photos of him. Emma wondered how they got the photos. How long had this party plan been happening without her knowing? Why weren't they including her? She was his wife, and they knew her well. They were her friends, at least until now. The whole party was absurdly strange.

Emma held her head up high, regal in her pearls, even though the insult was apparent to all. Under the surface of her carefully chosen dress, her blood began to boil.

As her husband's female students surrounded his table, Emma clearly saw all the ways they had replaced her. Some had replaced her by his side while he was teaching. Others had replaced her as his muses. Some had replaced her as his travel companions, and still others had replaced her on the board of advisors of their business. She remembered the time he came home and told her that Prudence wanted to have a baby, and she wanted him to be the daddy. Before Emma could even inquire how that could work out, she firmly said no.

She had been feeling the life seeping out of her marriage—and her place in the business they had built together—for some time. But on this day, it was more than a feeling. All the signs were abundantly clear.

Emma shook off her memory of the party and turned to the young bird. She knew that she and the female kestrel had a destiny together. She needed to respect that even more than the outcome of life or death. In a flash, a spiritual connection began, a story unfolding, each telling the other what she needed to know. The concept of freedom leaped beyond the boundaries of time and space. The souls of both Emma and the kestrel had already begun their journey together. The winds of change blew upon them, sending them into the hands of transformation. They would mother each other through what is eternal.

"What are our choices?" Emma asked the bird. "I could take you to the wildlife center, but your parents will lose you, and they will never know what happened to you. That doesn't feel right today.

"I can't put you back in your nest," Emma continued, "because it is impossible for me to reach, and you will fly out again anyway. And since we know the ravens ate your brother yesterday and whimsically spread his feathers around the arena, they would love the possibility to eat you today.

"So," she concluded, "I guess our only option is to build you another nest and give you some time to fully grow your feathers until you can fly on your own. Then you will be strong enough to fight your own demons."

With the decision made, the two walked the path to the barn. Emma turned one of the horse stalls into a giant nest so the parents could see and hear the baby and know she was okay. Emma left a small area open for the parents to go into the stall to feed their baby, but not big enough to let the hungry ravens in.

Over the next several days, Emma fed the kestrel while mother and father overlooked. After a few days, Emma opened the stall door during the day when the ravens were busy elsewhere so the baby's mom could feed her herself. She dutifully brought crickets and mouse heads to her hungry fledgling.

One day when Emma peered into the stall, she found no bird. The little one had flown out of her stall and was peacefully sitting atop a stack of hay. Emma quietly approached her, wondering if she would fly away. But she didn't. Looking into Emma's brown eyes, she waited and listened with eager attention as Emma quietly spoke.

"I don't think you are quite ready to be free yet," she said. "You have to be able to fly into the rafters to get away from those that want to eat you, dear one. How about we give you a few more days? If you can show me that you can get out of your stall over and over, you will be free to come and go as you choose. Then you will be ready to face your destiny and express your free will."

Emma offered her outstretched hand. The little one stepped daintily upon it, and the two walked in silence, each holding the other up, back to the stall that had become a nest.

The fledgling practiced leaving her nest for several more days until, one day, she was in the highest rafter. She was now free. Emma went about her daily routine of feeding the animals and smiled as she looked up into the rafters and found the bird looking down at her with a deep contentment for her fate. Her future was out of Emma's hands now; it was up to the fledgling to save herself.

Meanwhile, Emma couldn't help but wonder about her own life. Had she transformed her stall into a nest? Or was she still denying her own ability to set herself free? Who was her raven?

Deep in her heart, Emma knew that she was being hunted too. For a long time now, she had fed herself mice by living in her own fantasy that she was doing the right thing. She had continued to believe if she loved her husband enough, everything would be okay.

But was it the right thing to stay with a man who pecked at her, like a horse nipping and rearing, demonstrating power over her, intimidating the free spirit inside of her? The innocent child inside her wondered, *Why is this happening to me? Isn't the world supposed to be fair? Shouldn't everything be okay if only I do the right thing?*

But Raven had a message for Emma, too, and, one day, the feathered sorceress left it for her in a way that only nature can demand that you change your shape. She ate the little kestrel, beheaded her, and ceremoniously left her head in the middle of the arena.

The dainty feathers were scattered everywhere. Emma felt the dagger enter her heart as she knelt to pick up the feathered head. She knew her little spirit bird had been too peaceful. She had been too innocent to know that her life was in danger and that someone was out to feed their progeny with her essence. Emma hadn't anticipated that Raven would rub it in her face this way.

Emma turned and looked up at Raven perched in the rafters. Raven's presence looked ominous; her feathered robe glistened a brilliant black. Looking into her eyes, Emma asked, "Okay, what do you want me to see? What is the message you are trying to tell me?"

Raven spoke in a cackle-deep voice, "Wake up! *She is you!* You are in grave danger. If you do not take that robe off of your face and put it on your back, if you do not let go of your fantasy that the world you are living in is a fair place, you will be eaten too."

Emma did not like this answer. Oh no, she did not. "But I've done nothing wrong," she said. "Why are these dark forces against me?"

"It's because they do not understand you. They think you have too much power," Raven said. "They envy that you can live between the worlds of animals and humans. They cannot see that you have been chosen to bridge these two worlds and that you must remain wild to be true to your purpose here on earth. They do not like your wildness. They think you are a threat to their ego and pride. They are afraid you will see through their lies and pretense."

Raven continued more intensely now, "You see through the illusion of the human mind. When are you finally going to see that your freedom is required now? It is you who will send the message that humans need to admit their egoistic lack of respect for the Great Mother Earth. It's time for man to stop the folly of conquering all that is free. Stop the rape of the land, stop polluting the air, stop sucking the water out of the deep earth's surface. They must stop poisoning the soils and medicine plants inconveniently growing in their massive monocultures.

"Don't you see, if you are to meet your destiny, you must leave the one who wants to keep you boxed up in the stall? You must fly away from those who don't believe in you. If you do not stand up and fight for yourself, you will die."

"It can't be true that I will die," Emma said. "I am free inside of myself. Isn't that enough?"

"No, it's not enough. I may be your messenger, but you are also mine. This is your destiny, as much as it is mine. I need you to get out of the stall and set yourself free."

"I don't know how to do that," Emma said.

"Yes, you do!"

"Are you sure you are telling me the truth? Maybe I'm imagining all of this. After all, I am talking to you without words. The world I was raised in says that is impossible."

"My point exactly," Raven insisted.

Over the next few weeks, Emma could not stop thinking about this conversation. When she tried to deny this truth handed down to her by the black magician, Raven sat in the old pine tree and cawed at her open door. "Caw! Caw! Caw!" She filled Emma's home with her gruff voice and unrelenting cry: "I will not leave you alone! I will haunt you with my deep voice until you pay attention to me!"

As the sun peered above the far hills at the crack of dawn, Raven pecked at the wood porch outside Emma's bedroom door, waking her from her sleep. *Peck, peck, peck.* "Wake up!" she insisted. "Wake up! Wake up!"

The mother raven haunted Emma's every step. As she diligently began her daily chores of feeding the horses, Raven cawed at her from the rafters of the barn. "Caw! Caw!" Emma turned a corner, and there she was, dressed in black, sitting on the fence, yelling at her. As the day went along, Emma could hear the *caw* flying on the afternoon breeze, piercing her ears.

She tried to retreat under her prayer tree, only to find the ancient bird waiting for her there. "Caw! Caw! Caw! There will be no peace for you until you listen!"

Vainly, Emma tried to look in every direction but the one in front of her. She slumped onto an old tree stump in her private garden and tried to catch her breath. Finally, exhausted, she turned to the yelling raven. "*Okay!* What do you want me to see?"

"You know what there is to see."

"Oh, you think I should leave my husband? Is that what you are trying to tell me?" Emma yelled up at her.

Emma had avoided this question for years now. She had tried to tune out the times he'd told her, "I'm done with this marriage." She had believed that if you loved someone enough, everything would be okay.

But over the last several years, her heart had bled small drops of ruby-red blood onto the floor in her stall. Only recently had she realized that it was her own blood she was stepping in. Her heart had grown weak and sad.

"His destiny has been sitting on top of yours for years," said Raven. "Now it is time to set yourself free. We have all been trying to tell you this for a long time. That is why Golda came to you. That is why you will never forget Smiley. And what about the Titanic and Elsie? We're all here for you—rooting for you. And now this little fledgling female bird has given her life for you to retrieve yours. What else must be sacrificed before you take responsibility for your own life?" Raven was adamant now and frustrated at why Emma kept avoiding all of the messages from the spirit world.

"Get a grip, Emma!"

Raven finally had her full attention, and she didn't want to stop talking. "Do you remember the dream you had a few years ago? The house you were living in was being swept away by the raging waters from a broken dam below your pond. You walked into the house, and on the top of the cupboard was a black owl. She was amazing! She was so black and shiny. She was sitting on a nest. At first, you were scared. You knew there was no such thing as a black owl.

"*Have you come to haunt me?* you thought. But when you allowed yourself to feel her answer, she replied, 'I am the vision of a whole new reality—beyond the human mind. I am creativity, your imagination in full glory. I am birth—your birth when you are ready to see me.'

"Do you remember how that dream has followed you around? You keep wondering who the black owl is. You knew then, as you know now: she was foretelling what is yours to do now."

"But I can't do this," Emma protested. "I can't leave my husband. What about my kids? Where will I live?" Emma was profoundly disturbed. She had lived in the shadow of his magnificence for so long that she had forgotten she had her own two wings and her own thermal winds to ride.

But she knew Raven was right. She lowered her head and cried as Raven sat quietly by her side. After what seemed like an eternity, Emma felt a warm breeze on her cheek. For the first time in years, she wasn't scared. She felt the earth push her to her feet and caught the smell of sweet jasmine in the air, awakening her senses. She looked into Raven's eyes like a baby looks at its mother while nursing at her breast. "Thank you," she said.

Raven gently hopped onto her shoulder, and they walked in silence, following the breeze to the top of the hill where they could see the ocean through the tall grass.

The two were carried back to a time long ago when Emma was still a free spirit. When no one was around, her favorite pastime was to jump atop her flashy paint mare, Sumi (her friend, mother, and sister all rolled into one), and run through the field and bush up the hill overlooking the ocean. Emma's spirit was strong, connected to all life around her. She remembered how she kept her spirit free and untarnished from the negative grip of her mother's control. Now it was time to reconnect to her original self so that her intuition and animal senses could guide her free of human domination.

Finally, after all these years and hard work, she turned toward her fear. As she accepted her destiny, the sun began to shine, and her skin began to radiate with warmth. Her belly was on fire. She was in love with new possibilities.

And for the first time in months, Raven stopped cawing. Instead, she waited silently at the prayer tree, where she gave Emma strength. Even in the barn, cloaked in a chief's robe, Raven came down from the rafters and rested on the fence beside her. Everywhere Emma went, Raven was there, leading her onward.

"Thank you again," Emma whispered humbly, each time she saw Raven and felt her silent strength.

One night, she had a dream. It wasn't a visual dream; there was no story to it. Rather, a great flush of energy ran through her like the water that rushes to the ocean when the dam breaks. Surging through her, Raven was now in her body. She had become Raven, and the night had become day.

Emma's strength continued to grow as she accepted that the kind of flower she knew herself to be would never bloom in such shade. And so, with great sadness, she began preparing to leave her husband. Despite believing all the fairy tales of her youth, she finally understood her love for this man was not enough to save their marriage.

Now, she had to love *herself* enough to save herself. It was a matter of life or death.

Running

Running for your life
On the back of a wild horse, you ride
Through the brambled forest of night
As the ghosts of yesterday haunt your past,
Wanting your future.

The ancient path whispers,
"You will not fall, you will not falter,
You'll reach the moonlit meadow soon,

Dear one, soon."
With nothing on but
Your warrioress robe of deep maroon,
Shells adorning its seams
Shells you plucked off the sandy beach of yesterday
And sewn together ever so delicately.
To give you strength for this day.

Your horse is wild tonight!
He, too, is running for his life.
His neck outstretched, eyes wide and
Nostrils flared.
Your hair flows effortlessly behind you
Protecting you from the past
As you ride,
As you run
Toward the light of the silvery moon.

The storm's fierce wind
Erases the tears from your cheeks
As your hooves pound the dark umber dirt,
Carving a path
Through the dark moss and fallen leaves.

Your hearts beating as one
Each saving the other.
Each breathing the same breath,
The same air.

Time falls away,
Yesterday is gone
Tomorrow will be here soon
While the moon begins to glow upon you
Warming your faces
Reaching toward the meadow of tomorrow.

"You will not fall,
You will not falter,
You will arrive.
Soon, dear one, soon,"
The ancient path whispers before you.

Opportunities and Contemplations

REFLECTION

Raven *did* come to me. Not only was my little kestrel slain, but fifteen of my hens were massacred overnight. I finally had no choice but to look into my fear.

Other lives, "she" lives, were at stake now. I was no longer willing to let others suffer because I didn't want to deal with what was no longer working in my life. I felt like my little kestrel girl and my chicken ladies had been killed to send me one last plea to listen to the messages that nature had been offering all around me. Whether that is true or not, I know I have witnessed firsthand the domination of women (and animals). I imagine others have seen much worse.

While this is not the main topic of this book, there is something to be said about Mother Nature, the feminine power, the masculine domination of the last few hundred years, what women feel and know in their bones, and why we need to stand tall now more than ever.

We can glean lessons from nature to find our way; we have to listen. And even though I am of the land, it took me a long time to acknowledge what I was listening to. I hope my confession helps you listen fervently and take a stand sooner and faster than I did.

WHAT DO YOU NEED TO TAKE A STAND FOR?

- Are you letting your spirit be your guide?
- Are you listening?
- Is someone in your life trying to get your attention? What do you hear when you listen?
- Does the line, "The flower she knew herself to be would never bloom in such shade" strike a chord in you? What is shading you from your own full expression?
- What are you sacrificing in yourself to accommodate your old story?
- Where do you need to take a stand now?

TIME IN NATURE CONTEMPLATION

Find a quiet place in nature to be by yourself. It's time to let go of what no longer serves you.

Take something with you that represents what you no longer need, perhaps an old story. Find a place to give it back to the Great Mother. She can recycle it and give it new energy.

One Day She Finally Knew

For nineteen years, Emma was a devoted wife. She mopped the floors, tended the garden, grew flowers, planted fruit trees, hosted parties for his friends, mothered his children, and fed him well. It was never enough.

When Ken was away on business for a week or two at a time, her relationships with her kids were great. Everyone seemed balanced and happy. But when he came home, Emma noticed that the kids teased her and made fun of her. Her son seemed to take great pleasure in criticizing Emma so his dad would get in a good laugh. At first, it seemed like everyone was having a good time. Emma tried to defend herself, which only made things worse. Doing the dishes distracted her from her hurt feelings.

Emma and her husband had planned to take their middle daughter to an amazing astrologer known for her psychic knowing powers. As Emma readied herself for the long journey to the city, he announced, "I have decided that this is a father-daughter outing."

"But she is my daughter, too, and I was so looking forward to going." She tried not to sound desperate. She argued with him to no avail and finally gave up. She put her tail between her legs and went outside to cry.

When father and daughter came home, they were optimistic and excited about her reading. Emma wanted to learn more about what the astrologer had said. They replied with superficial enthusiasm, not really including Emma in their special day.

Emma listened to their story of the astrologer's tale on a cassette they brought home, wishing she had been there to witness her daughter's experience. The astrologer's interpretations of her daughter were so profound that Emma decided to listen to the recording of the astrologer's session with her husband from his visit to her several months earlier. He had left his recording on the counter and dismissively said, "If you want to listen, go ahead."

As she listened to the tape, she heard another woman's voice, not the astrologer's, but a woman who was there to share the experience with her husband. "Say more," she said. It was Prudence.

Emma's heart sank. As her thoughts spun, she heard him say, "I want to talk about my relationship. Well, yes, my relationship because I am done." The words fell into Emma's lap like the red bricks she had envisioned on her coffin. His recorded voice of months earlier rang through her delicate ears as random thoughts flashed before her: *He took Prudence to his reading? Why was she there and not me? I remember how he didn't want me to go with him. I think my world is falling apart. Oh my god. Oh my god. Maybe, just maybe, I am not crazy after all. Maybe something else has been going on; something is being hidden from me?* Emma felt as if she had been dealt a traumatic blow to her delicate cheek. She had taken blows before, but this one was too much to turn the other cheek.

She remembered the night, many moons ago, when he had returned home from a teaching trip in Montana. She poured him a glass of her wine, which she had made the previous year, and couldn't wait to hear how his trip went. As he rose the glass of ruby wine to his lips, she saw another ring on his wedding ring finger. It was silver with a red stone. Emma took a grounding breath and, without much thought, curiously asked, "Where did you get that ring on your wedding finger?"

"Oh, this ring?" He smiled, happily pushing it in her face. "A woman gave it to me. I've always wanted a ring like this."

"A woman gave it to you?" Emma asked politely, pushing away the dark abyss in front of her.

"Yes. And, no, I did not have an affair with her."

Emma's mind struggled to find the next words. *Another woman?* She hadn't entertained the possibility he could be having an affair. Why did he even bring it up? She was in shock. But she had been trained well. Don't get upset, don't get angry. Just very reasonably ask, "And what is it doing on your wedding finger?"

"Oh, my wedding ring got too small. Didn't you know that?"

"No, you should have told me. I could have had it resized or a new one made for you."

A few days later, she learned of a company board meeting happening in four days. Several of the board of advisors were flying in, including Prudence. The company was paying their airfare and lodging fees, and no one, not even her husband, had bothered to tell her when it was happening.

"Hey, I just found out there is a board meeting this Saturday in Bodega Bay. What time is it? I'd like to come," she stated as if everything was fine and dandy. This was indeed her last effort to go along with the inequity she knew was happening.

"You can't come. Prudence won't have it. She said if you come, she won't be on the board anymore."

Emma got upset. "I am your wife. This is my company too. I have a right to be at the meeting. What time is it?"

"No. You can't come."

It no longer mattered that she was his wife and the mother of his children. It no longer mattered that she had made this business for him. And it no longer mattered that she had made him all the money he had asked for. She could barely stand up. Once again, she felt like Smiley, all beaten up and standing there stoic, waiting for the next lash.

Inside, she was angry. She was upset. Had that been how Smiley felt? If he had shown it, he would have been beaten for that as well. His skin had grown callous. Emma pretended she couldn't be hurt either.

Part of her wanted to rage, to turn herself into a fire-breathing dragon and unleash the dragon's fiery breath upon the land, igniting the dry, brittle grasses of yesterday.

Instead, she took a deep breath and looked at the evidence. Prudence had gone on the river trips with Ken and her kids. Trips that were supposed to be family vacations. She went to places like Montana to be his protégé student because they had decided that Emma shouldn't so she could stay home and take care of the kids. Now Prudence had taken over her position on the advisory board of her own business. And she gave him a ring to replace her ring on his wedding ring finger?

"How many signs do you need?" Raven sent her call into the late summer breeze.

Raven was right. Emma had lost. Being angry and avoiding the cards in front of her was not a good survival strategy.

That night, she had a terrible dream. She was pushed off a cliff. She grabbed a branch as her feet scrabbled for the ground. The branch broke as her screams rang through the canyon. She lost all footing and fell into the unknown terror of silence.

As she fell headfirst into the dark abyss, her good luck pennies and fairy teeth fell from her pockets and hurtled down to the rigid rocks below. Her power necklace broke and plunged down into the lost sea. She scrambled with raptor claws to catch it, but to no avail. The harsh waves were ready to take her home as she fell toward the black waters. All was lost. Emma crashed into the waves, unconscious. She floated listlessly for what seemed like an eternity.

After all reality had abandoned her, a white wave from far across the sea with a horse's mane of silvery steam crashed into her nostrils, forcing stinging shards of life back into her lungs. She gagged on the salty water as she clawed at the sea, grasping for her life. She gasped for air. The wispy mane of the wave pushed her to the wave's crest.

Emma was no longer the woman she had been. The silent horse on ocean waves had slammed her original self up her nose with a salty sting and willed her back to life. Her original self, like a newborn babe, bobbed in the ocean for weeks, a boat unmoored, no land in sight. Slowly, she remembered who she was and, one morning, let the now-mellow waves take her back to shore.

The sand crunched between her toes as she walked purposefully home. She was no longer angry. She was no longer hoping, groping, or begging for her husband to return to her. She no longer tried to save the love flowers that lay dying in the garden.

No More

You will not dominate me anymore
Not upon any shore.

You will not take my spirit
Will not spoil my warrioress robe
With your tainted fingers
Your desperate probe.

You will not force your way into my wounded heart
You will not stay.

Go, go now, you fool
I will not be your ego's tool
Feel your pain deep inside
Don't punish me on every ride.

Learn a lesson
Learn it well
You have lost me forever now.

I will not let you enter me,
Invade my space or take from me
I will attack your disrespect
With my legs and fiery breath
Hot and furious upon your face
I will not be disgraced.

So, go, go now, you fool
And take your charming smile
Lying eyes and heartless wile
Feel your pain deep inside
Let go of your selfish pride.

Learn a lesson
Learn it now
I will be the change
I will walk with grace
And without shame.

Opportunities and Contemplations

REFLECTION

While it was a long time coming, once I was ready to protect myself rather than defend my virtues, the decision to separate from my husband came quickly and without much thought. Yet, I was worried about my children. I had promised them that their parents would always stay married. I believed that. Now, I knew I had to break that promise, not only to survive but to hopefully teach them what a more balanced relationship between a woman and a man could be like. I hoped that someday they would understand why I needed to break away from their father.

I always believed that marriage was a lifelong commitment. But I also knew that I was walking on a road toward my death. I needed to live for my children. I needed to end the legacy of dominance and subordinacy in my family roots. And I needed to find a new way to be an empowered woman.

I didn't know what the future looked like. But I did know I would no longer accept the role of pleasing others to my own detriment. I trusted my intuition to guide me through the destruction of a life I had built and believed in for so long. I felt in line with my destiny, even though it created tremendous pain for my precious children and me.

WHERE IS YOUR "NO"?

- Is there a place in your life now where you need to take a stand for yourself?
- Or, is there a place in your past where you were disrespected, and you no longer accept that as your truth? You can still take a stand and say, "No more."
- What is the statement you want to make, the stake in the ground that says, "No more"?

TIME IN NATURE CONTEMPLATION

Every day for a week, make time to go outside to a quiet spot where you can be alone. Give yourself permission to take this time for yourself without apology or stipulations. What moods or feelings emerge? Be in the moment, let whatever wants to visit and inform you to be present. There is no need to fix or determine, no need to resolve or divide. Just be.

Coyote Freedom

The fog was thick and moist as it clung to the meadows. It was only seven in the morning, and coffee was on.

As Emma prepared for her morning chores, Ken came into the house hurriedly and said, "There is a coyote stuck in the fence in the far field."

Emma's ears instantly perked forward. "Where?"

"The far west fence," Ken said as he headed toward his closet.

"Aren't you going to do something?" Emma asked.

"I have a call to make," he replied, and off he went.

How can you leave a coyote stranded in a fence? Emma thought as she threw on some jeans and her mud boots. On her way out, she grabbed some gloves and wire cutters. She looked to the western horizon and saw what appeared to be a coat draped across the fence. She looked more closely. No, it wasn't a coat. It was a coyote. His body was laced in the top rung of the hog-wire fence that kept the neighbor's cows on the other side.

The coyote's foot was caught in a trap designed to strangle the predator, but instead, it had snared his leg. In an effort to escape, he had tried to jump over the fence, then through it until he had threaded himself like a macramé bracelet in the wires and was stuck hanging like a rag doll in the air.

"Wow, you've sure gotten yourself into quite a mess, haven't you?" Emma said as she approached. "You know, my neighbors would kill you right now if they saw you here. That is their very intention. And if they find out I am going to cut you out of the fence, we will both be in trouble."

Exhausted by his attempts to escape the human's trap, the coyote looked at her quietly. Emma knew how to rescue injured animals and to let them know that she was there to help them.

"Okay, I'll make you a deal," she said. "If I cut you out of this fence, will you promise me that you and your family will not kill my sheep?"

"Okay," was all the tired coyote had the strength to reply.

"I am going to cut you out of the fence, little by little. It is going to take some time, and you have to stay perfectly still."

The coyote looked into Emma's deep brown eyes, and an understanding grew between them. Emma started by cutting the snare from the coyote's back leg and then the two wires that ensnared his other back leg. Then she gently placed her hand on the side of the coyote to cut the wire under his belly without cutting his skin. She had to cut each wire in a specific order so the coyote wouldn't end up falling and hanging himself.

Ten minutes later, the last wire to cut was right next to the coyote's mouth. He had been so quiet. He had not made a sound—not even a growl.

"Remember the deal we made," Emma said as she cut the last wire. Her hand brushed against the coyote's muzzle as he fell to the ground.

Emma stepped back a few steps to give the coyote room to orient himself back to the earthly plane. He very slowly walked away, turning several times to look back at Emma as if to say, "Thank you," even though he was a bit embarrassed that he had gotten caught.

"Remember our deal," Emma called out softly.

"Yes, I will," he whispered as he disappeared into the grasses behind the thickets and into the valley below.

A lot of people thought of Coyote as a trickster. But Emma knew that Coyote had come into her life at this time to challenge her decisions. She had already filed separation papers. Things were still strained between them, but they had been together for nineteen years. They had a habit of relating to one another to coordinate family, business, and ranch matters. Liam was still a pup at nine years old, and Mae was heading off to college in the fall.

In her heart, Emma had decided to end the marriage, and yet, the tremendous ramifications of such a decision were daunting. She loved her husband, but her spirit was entangled in the fence—like Coyote—and Ken either chose not to see it or didn't care.

It no longer mattered what he thought. She knew she had to cut herself out of the trap she was in, just like she had done for Coyote.

That night, Coyote's spirit taunted her in the quiet before she fell asleep. "You were not afraid of me," Coyote whispered in the dark stillness. "So why are you so afraid to cut yourself out of the fence you have woven yourself into? You look like a ragamuffin, all tangled in that fence, just like your mother used to say."

Emma tossed and turned. "That is not fair!"

Coyote's spirit went on. "You sit by yourself weeping, feeling sorry for yourself. But do you see how easy it was for you to come to my rescue, to cut me out of the fence? You know this was not an accident. You know the lesson. You know your path, but are you willing to choose it? I shouldn't have to do it for you. You must cut yourself out of the fence. I am you, girl."

Emma tossed and turned. Her dreams were dark and murky. She wanted them to go away, but she respected Coyote too much to ignore him.

"Maybe you should stay in your misery," he said. "Go ahead and complain how life is not treating you fairly. You know you could trick yourself into staying in your old story and repeating your pain over and over again."

"If you choose the new path, you know all too well the vast unknown walks with you. What's the big deal? Are you scared of the lack of sureness, the risk of failure? What is a life lived in the safety of your self-imposed walls of reason?"

"Stop already!" Emma cried as she twisted the tangled bedsheets in her hands.

Coyote's spirit had one last question for her: "Did you free me?" he asked. "Or did I free you?"

Emma awoke the next morning knowing in her heart that to grasp her freedom, she had to cut herself out of the entanglement of old patterns. Coyote's spirit didn't care where she was going; he wanted her to cut herself loose so she could follow her intuition and trust the mystery of her life. He knew she deserved to be set free.

Coyote You

Coyote you, coyote me
Trickster known to be
Coyote you, coyote me
Shall I set you free?

Strung up in the fence
Your grey red coat cold and wet
Your eyes a wild sight
Though you never show your fright.

Coyote you, coyote me
Shall I set you free?

How'd you get up in that fence?
Trapped in your own defense
Biting that wire the neighbor set
Not meant to keep you as a pet
But rather kill you dead
The wire wrapped around your head.

Let your humor out to play
There's always another way
Within you, within me

Together, free, we'll walk the land
Protecting it from the bad man
Who doesn't know another way to pray
To simply ask in an honorable way
To respect nature's way

Coyote you, coyote me
Promise me if I set you free
You'll spare my sheep
Protect them like Little Bo-Peep.

Coyote you, coyote me
And now I set you free
Free to you and free to me.

Opportunities and Contemplations

REFLECTION

What can I say about the coyote stuck in the fence? I cut him out and set him free. The metaphor was profound, especially at this time in my life. I cut the coyote out of his entrapment, the entrapment set by man; I gave him life instead of death. Who was doing that for me?

Maybe people call coyotes tricksters because they do not understand that the coyote appears on one's path to offer a choice right when you have decided to do something different. Coyote comes at the fork in your path, taunting you. "Are you sure you want to walk down the new path? Wouldn't it be easier to stay on the road you are on?"

Now I say, "Thank you, Coyote, for pointing the way. I see the old path before me and the new path, and while the old path looks so familiar, I must choose the new path." Coyote replies, "It's not so much to challenge a new opportunity, but to make sure you know you are really choosing, really determined to step onto the new path." Coyote tempts the newcomer with the illusions of the old path to challenge your resolve.

This moment with the coyote changed my perspective. It was as if I was finally setting myself free from the snares of the old paradigms. Particularly poignant to me was the old paradigm that my neighboring ranchers, all of them men, simply kill coyotes. So, of course, coyotes kill their lambs. It is a vicious cycle.

After that day and the new agreement I had made with the coyote, my sheep were never killed by coyotes again. I had a coyote family living in my pastures, but they did not hunt my lambs.

The local male neighbors were heard whispering over coffee during their early morning ritual at the old market in town. "How come she doesn't have coyote problems, and we do?"

Coyote and I have kept our secret, and I dare never tell them. After all, I am just a girl rancher. And now I'll add "in their eyes."

GIVE YOURSELF A SECOND CHANCE

I'm going to let you roll with this one. Here are questions to consider: Is the coyote mirroring my domestication, as in, "I am woven into the fence?" Or is the coyote me talking to myself, saying, "I need to set you free; we can make a new agreement." Let your mind wander; journal without editing. Flow freely.

TIME IN NATURE CONTEMPLATION

Take time in nature to breathe. If you can find a forest nearby, a desert, or the sea, breathe in the aromatic fragrances. Let your spirit self be free. Imagine you are cutting yourself out of the fence. Let your legs and arms flex and stretch. Yawn, howl, let the air move through you. Declare what you are "done with." What new agreements do you want to make for yourself, you "child of nature"?

Taking a Stand

Emma was ready to be misunderstood. She stopped wishing someone would save her. No one had ever come to her defense before; why would they now? She knew it was up to her to save herself. She knew she needed to stop protecting her husband's identity at the expense of her well-being. It was time to stop pretending that her life was not in crisis.

The morning after she set the coyote free, Emma took the kids to school and tidied the kitchen, like she always did. She went down to the barn to work with the nameless horse who reminded her of Golda.

She groomed her in the usual routine, saddled her, and took her into the arena to lunge her. She couldn't feel this horse's heart. It was as if she had no will, no life; she was an empty shell of a horse. Every time Emma tried to make a move to ride her, she got fidgety and anxious, more than a normal unbroken horse would do.

Emma stopped the horse from going around in circles. "What is it, girl?" she whispered. "You seem so far away. I can't feel you. Talk to me."

Emma rested her head on the lonely horse's neck, closed her eyes, and breathed quietly. She had a vision. She saw this chestnut mare when she was a little filly. She was a happy girl. But one day, people came and took her away from her mother. They pushed her into a big white box and closed all the doors so she couldn't see anything. She was screaming wildly for her mother. Her eyes were white with terror, and she broke into a terrible sweat.

The mare's mother and all the horses were screaming and running frantically back and forth in the paddock, trying to jump over the fence to find her. They could hear her, but they couldn't see her. Their hooves on the dry dirt scratched the earth, and the dust rose so they could no longer even see the big white box.

The lady who had been her human was nowhere to be found. She loved that lady named Sarah. Where was she? All of a sudden, the big box started moving, bumping, and throwing her around in the black wilderness of nowhere. She tossed and turned, whinnied, and cried for hours and hours. By the time it stopped, she was exhausted. She was dripping with sweat; her whole body was shaking uncontrollably. The whites of her eyes were stretched with terror.

The mare lowered her head. Emma could see a few tears in her eyes. Emma wept too. The two wounded girls wept together.

"I miss my mother," said the mare. "I miss Sarah too. I don't know where they are. And this new lady, Mindy, wants you to train me to ride. But my body is broken. It hurts to canter. I don't want anyone to ride me; it hurts too much."

"Now I get it," Emma said, relieved to finally understand what she had been feeling in the blank void between what Mindy wanted and what this mare could do. "Thank you for telling me."

Emma had already known that this horse didn't want to be ridden, but she'd doubted her intuition. Instead, she had been sticking to the old horse training rule she'd been taught: make the horse do what you want. If she'd gone to this horse's owner and simply said, "Your horse doesn't want to be ridden," she'd look incompetent.

"I knew something was wrong," Emma told the mare. "I didn't feel good pressuring you the way I have been—the way I'm paid to do. Let's stop this right now. Let's start again. Tell me your name."

The mare lifted her head with a new light in her eye. "Emma, my name is Rose."

"That is one of my favorite names! It's perfect. I shall call you Rose. And I am going to tell your owner that I am concerned about riding you because I think something is wrong. Something is hurting in your body, which is why you have been resistant. I'm also going to tell her that you are lonely because you were taken from your family and that she needs to bond with you and become your friend. How's that?"

"I like it." Rose licked her lips with joy.

Later that day, Emma spoke to Mindy and shared her concerns. She recommended a vet visit to examine Rose's physical body. Mindy agreed.

Emma felt relieved inside. She had been scared to take a stand with the owner, but she knew she had to. She felt out of integrity with Rose to keep pushing her rather than being curious about why the horse was resistant.

It was a big moment for Emma as a horse trainer. This was another reason why Golda had come to her. Emma knew she needed to listen now.

She found an old, half-broken wooden chair beside the tack room and sat outside in the afternoon breeze. Her attention wandered to the estero down below. She felt far away from the waters, yet she could feel the water molecules of the tide moving through her sinews.

"Why do we humans think all horses need to be ridden?" she asked her spirit friends. "Why do we think this is their sole purpose in life, the only value they have?"

She sat for a while and listened. "The stand I need to take for Rose is the stand I need to take for myself," she realized. "Why is this so hard for me to do for myself?"

The quiet, wise woman inside her replied: "You've been protecting his identity for too long. Taking a stand for yourself means the end of your marriage. It breaks the illusion of unity you once had. You will be the one to blame. You will be ostracized from the very community you created. You will be cut off. You won't have your children with you all the time as you do now."

"It's so hard to bear," said Emma. "I can't stand the thought of not being there for my children all the time. I am so worried about them. Will I be able to stay here? If not, where will I live? There are so many unknowns." She sighed. The invisible ropes that had been tightening around her started to go slack.

The breeze swept up the grassy hills carrying the salty undertones of the estero as if to say, "We're all here for you, dear one."

Emma felt a quiet resolve rise within her. The stand she needed to take now was not one of defiance. It was a stand to be taken out of defeat. But it wasn't a bad defeat. It was a surrender she needed to take to set herself free.

Her spirit self took over, despite all her resistance. Her logical mind was no longer in control. Her worries about what others would think were carried away in the breeze and traveled to faraway shores so she could no longer hold onto them.

She went home and pulled out her sketchbook, dusted it off, and let her intuition guide the way. She drew illustration after illustration of a young woman and her spirit horse in nature. In the pictures, there were trees, flowers, water, and even a spider. In each drawing, the girl and the horse were grounded and confident. They were strong but not fierce. They were united. Nothing could tear them apart.

She finally accepted who she was. She knew what she had to do. She was ready to step into the next unknown future with her warrioress robe firmly over her shoulders and her pearls and shells in her pockets. She called on Raven, Golda, and Smiley to stay with her. She asked Coyote to guide her through the darkness whenever she lost sight of her freedom waiting on the other side. Keoki was also by her side.

She hoped that someday her children would understand what she had to do. She walked up to the house a different woman.

Trusting

A new day is born.
A time of change.
Is it the unknown that unnerves me,
Or is it the stillness within a day?

My mind is quiet
Yet my heart pounds fiercely.
Where is the solid earth upon which I must stand?

Or do I just allow myself to be moved by the oceanic tide of my life,
Trusting its ebb and flow?
Trusting its ebb and flow.

Opportunities and Contemplations

REFLECTION

There were many assaults on my feminine power during this time, and they were coming one after the other. None of them made sense. The dam I had built to stop the water's flow was truly broken. My intuition took over by sending me to my sketchbook.

At the time, I didn't understand why I had to draw. But I was determined. Every afternoon before dinner, I sat down at the dining room table and drew until everyone started coming home for dinner.

My unconscious mind was at work. I was drawing myself as the grounded warrioress, peaceful, but not to be dominated anymore. I imagined how I would want any young woman to feel: to embody her power, her beauty, even her sensuality, without embarrassment or apology.

My intuition even tricked my logical mind into participating by focusing on the purpose of the illustrations: to be made into a coloring book to share with young women coming of age. By coloring in the illustrations, I hoped they, too, would feel their inner power, beauty, and strength.

By taking a stand for Rose, I broke one of the old rules passed down for many generations, one of the fundamental rules of domination—to make another do as you wish. An unspoken rule in horsemanship "states" that once you ask the horse to do something, it must be done. You have to make the horse do it no matter what. I didn't have the heart to make Rose do something that was clearly painful for her because I had been hired to do so.

I talked to Mindy and told her I would not make Rose be ridden, that something was wrong within her body. I had the vet come out, and sure enough, she had suffered an injury before the age of two, where most likely she had been tied up at too young of an age when her body was still growing.

Rose had struggled fiercely to get free. In doing so, she had pulled a system of muscles and tendons, damaging an area around the neck vertebrae that caused chronic pain down the spine through her croup. No wonder she didn't want to be ridden.

Since then, I have seen this condition a number of times with people who come to me because they don't understand why their horse is being so resistant and won't allow them to be ridden. Some old horsemanship models tie young horses up and sack them out (meaning, scare them on purpose) so they pull back and learn they cannot get away. I've never done such horrid things to horses, nor have I ever seen it done. But I know that method has a long history in some antiquated horsemanship models. And I have assisted a lot of horses who had such tragic experiences to recover from their trauma.

So, whether Rose was sacked out or injured in the trailer (the big white box) is unknown. But the vet confirmed she should not be ridden. I suggested to Mindy that she send her back to the previous owner, Sarah, who was Mindy's sister. Sarah could give her a home and companionship. Mindy had been the one who thought her sister shouldn't have the horse because she didn't want to ride her. And so, Rose returned to her family.

If I hadn't set myself free from worrying about what the owner would think of me by telling her I wouldn't train her horse to ride, Rose might have had a terrible life. Unbeknownst to me at the time, I was already breaking the rules, cutting the invisible ropes of domestication that I shared with these horses.

WHAT DOES IT MEAN FOR YOU TO BE FREE?

- What old paradigms or rules are tying you up?
- What does your spirit self want to say to you?
- Are you letting your spirit self speak?
- Are you listening?

TIME IN NATURE CONTEMPLATION

Take some time in nature. Find a quiet place without people, if you can. Share with your nature friends, or if you have horses, with your horses, affirmations, such as "I am free! Totally free."

Declare, "I don't care what other people think of me. I AM WILD AND FREE."

Do it even if it doesn't feel heartfelt yet; it will someday.

The Last Stone Unturned

Emma tried one last attempt to save her marriage. She didn't want to leave any stone unturned. She asked Ken to go to therapy with her. Sometimes he agreed to come with her. She wanted a witness, a therapist who would be impartial, to help them figure out why they were so off with each other. The therapist was a good listener in many ways, but after a few sessions, Emma wasn't sure she could rely on him.

She sensed that the therapist was enamored with Ken and his mastery of somatics. The therapist wanted to show Ken he knew somatics too. There were other distractions during their sessions as well. He spoke about how he and his wife shared the same age difference as Emma and Ken. He often veered away from the point of the process to ask Ken how he dealt with their age difference. Then the therapist would talk about his own marriage. This felt weird to Emma. *Here we go again, two men like two turkeys ruffling their feathers together*, she thought. *Am I crazy? Am I invisible? Do I have no merit, no value? Am I being a whiny complaining bitch? What is going on?*

When she brought it up with Ken on the drive home, he didn't see anything weird about it. Emma felt the same craziness wash over her, seeing things that were wrong that others did not see. Something had changed, though. She saw through the veil of illusion that she was not wrong in what she could see. Her clients hired her because she could see things they could not, and they respected her for her ability. But Ken, who had once adored her for her unique way of seeing, had been shunning her for years. And she had allowed it.

At what would become their last session, Emma attempted once more to be heard and understood.

"It feels like the beginning of the end of our marriage started when Ted unleashed his tirade. It really hurts me that you didn't stand up for me. I am asking you to apologize to me for not standing up for me in our marriage and in our business."

He responded, "I thought you stood up for yourself just fine."

"That is not the point." Emma reached deep inside her vulnerability and continued, "I need you to stand up for me—not only to Ted but also to Prudence. Can't you see their deceit? Can't you see how they are trying to tear us apart? Things started to go bad between us when they came into our lives. Can't you see that?" She wanted so desperately for him to console her and tell her she was right and that he could see the truth in what she was saying.

Instead of supporting Emma, the therapist interjected, "You know, Emma, you go between being the victim and being the accuser."

Emma felt instantly shamed. Both scenarios sounded bad. Her body started to shake, and the only way she could ground herself was to look at the patterns of symmetry on the wallpaper. Her spirit self took over, grabbed her purse off the floor by the couch, stood tall, and she stated, "I will not be shamed anymore," and walked out the door.

She was fighting a losing battle. It was time to stop trying to get Ken to see why she was upset and in pain. It was time to stop asking for respect. She was exhausted from fighting for her dignity. Her point of view was not only ignored; it was degraded with a subtle hint of shame. The last vestiges of her respect for Ken started to slough off her skin, like dried sand that no longer lived by the ocean and needed to be returned to the dirt for recycling.

Like a full moon lights the darkest night, her dilemma was finally illuminated in a way she could see into the prison of her own making. How long had she turned his disrespect toward her into a vicious cycle of self-damnation? She had been trained well by her mom to believe there was no use in fighting for her dignity and self-respect. She had been conditioned like the domesticated horses in her life to take the psycho-spiritual abuse. There was no use fighting to free herself from the lashing. The quicker she gave up, the less pain there would be.

But those beliefs were no longer true. Her spirit self no longer agreed! Oh no, she did not.

The next morning before dawn, Emma woke startled and shaking. She jumped out of bed as if a poisonous snake was about to bite her. Her heart pounded like an ancient drummer, pounding harder and faster. It was time—no more excuses and no more waiting for him to listen.

She put pen to paper and wrote a letter to Ken. She tried to be graceful and understanding, not to plead or try any further to change the tide. She acknowledged that he was done with the marriage. She acknowledged that maybe their destiny together was complete. They had made beautiful children and a business that took care of people in such a meaningful way. She put it on his computer and went about getting the kids up and off to the county fair to show their animals.

Ken called at ten that morning to see how the kids were doing.

"They are having a great time. Lily got first place with her dairy goats," Emma happily reported, pretending nothing was wrong. She waited to see if he would say anything about the letter. After a few minutes, she asked, "Did you get the letter I left on your computer?"

"Yes, I did," was all he said. No other comment. Nothing like, "Wow, let's talk." Again, she felt shunned that he didn't even acknowledge he had received her letter. She'd had to ask.

The next day, Emma filed for divorce. She had hoped to talk with Ken and figure out together how they would unwind their life.

Ken acted like he was surprised Emma filed for divorce, yet he had ignored her requests to talk about what was happening. When he was home, he walked by her as if she wasn't there. He took the kids on outings without her. It didn't matter to Emma anymore; she knew what had to be done.

The tension in the house was thicker than black mud. Emma finally asked him to move out.

"No, I won't do that," he declared and continued to go about his business.

"I need some space. I am so mixed up right now. Maybe if you give me some space, we can figure things out," she pleaded.

The horses looked at her, not knowing what to do. Keoki came to her in the silence between her breaths. "You're not surprised, right? You knew he wasn't going to leave of his own accord."

Ken eventually moved into the studio in the left wing of the house, where he lived for another six months. He finally found a place by the coast, and for the first time in her life, Emma's children weren't with her for a week at a time. She struggled when her children were not home.

She felt guilty for breaking up the family. But every time she tried to think of another way to keep the family together, her spirit self reminded her she had run out of options. She knew this part would be hard—that is why she endured the pain for as long as she had. But it was far more painful than she had imagined.

Emma tried to stay focused on her future for her and her children. She could only hope the future would give her children a new perspective regarding how women deserve to be respected. She dreamed her girls would someday be able to stand for their dignity in better ways than she had been able to do, and her son would respect women in a way not modeled by his father.

Once word of her divorce got around, some of the locals became more restrained around her. Divorce wasn't common in that area at that time. It was as if the local women were afraid she might steal their husbands now that she was a single woman. Most of their mutual friends through the business chose to stay friends with Ken rather than Emma since they felt they needed to choose one side over the other. She had already been ostracized by the staff at the institute.

One of the institute's master coaches told her that Prudence had spread rumors that Emma and Ken had broken up because Emma "wasn't doing her self-work." In the small field of self-development, the worst thing a person can do is not "do their work." This couldn't have been further from the truth for Emma. Inside, she knew that she had done the hard work of developing herself and standing up for her right to be free, even if others didn't see it that way.

When she went to the kids' sports games at school, parents who used to be her friends spoke to each other in hushed voices, looking at her all the while. Through it all, Emma stood tall, smiled, and focused on her children.

At night when the kids were gone, she went down to the deck on the pond and wailed, an ancient cry that only a mother can make. She wept and wept over their absence. The night sky absorbed her motherly cries and sent fresh air to her tired lungs.

A New Day

The half-moon peered through the leaves of the trees above her.
The sky a soft steel blue, as the setting sun clung to the last plateau
just above the sea's beginning.
Ah, a clear night is coming, she thought.

She sat quietly on the ground,
The cool grass on warm soil holding up her frame.
A lone vulture glided by on its way home.
The air listened with silent patience,
Holding her up with its invisible stiffness.

The children were gone.
She didn't know what to do,
She didn't know when they would be home.
A few tears ran down her face
Hoping nobody would notice her pain.

Just as she was about to fall into the lonely abyss,
The call of a distant peacock rang over the hilltop
Settling beside her like a flute
Inviting her to follow its song of love.
The wind, connecting earth to air,
Dried her tears, all the time asking her to dance its dusky dance.
A bat called its funny "clack, clack, clack."
Knocking on the familiar door of dark, "clack, clack, clack,"
Reminding her that she was not alone
As the day turned into night.

She knew they were right.
She still had plenty of songs to sing
Love to share.
Feeling better, she stood up and stretched like a waking cat
Reaching toward the moon as if to touch its soft embrace.

Ready to face the unknown landscape of darkness,
She took one last glance across the dark umber hills before her.
Just then, a bobcat dressed in gold sprung from the grasses,
Full of opportunity and grace.
All was confirmed now
Even though it appeared dark all around her,
The mysterious moon and all its creatures of night
Heard her love song,
Welcoming her into her new home
And so, she entered the dark house, ready to dream her new day.

Opportunities and Contemplations

REFLECTION

Until this time, I believed when someone I loved said something about me that was "off" or "not right," then I must be wrong. I must be the one who is lacking in some way. The more I tried to understand why this craziness was happening to me, rather than saying "phooey" as most people would, the more lost I felt.

Ultimately, I filed for divorce. My logical mind didn't make the appointment. My spirit self dialed the phone and drove me to the lawyer's office. I started the wheels in motion to set myself free. I was on my way to the place that always remembered my name.

STOP THE SHAMING

- Are you blaming and shaming yourself for being different from the way others want you to be? What is at stake if you continue to degrade yourself this way?
- Enough is enough. Write down all the blame, shame, and the wrongs you or others have said you have done. Write them down as historical endings. Now cross them all out with a big black Sharpie as you say the words, "Oh no, you do not say those things to me anymore. You are no longer allowed in my space." Make a fire and burn the paper in a ceremony to stop the self-abuse.

TIME IN NATURE CONTEMPLATION

Take a walk in nature. Talk to Mother Earth. She has been hurt; she has been disrespected. Ask her, "How have you overcome that?"

Think of your walk as a "historical ending." Say to the nature around you, "I am done with those old storylines." If you have a lot of emotion about it, say it over and over again until the emotion subsides.

Stand tall, say your name, "I am _____, I stand tall, without apology. I am a child of you. Please show me the way to my freedom. You are me, and I am you. Show me a simple way. Thank you. Thank you for your frankness."

Cancer and the Workhorse

Months turned into years, and Emma and Ken finally resolved their dissolution. He got the ranchette closer to town, and she got the horse ranch. He retained the well-established, profitable business—the financial asset that was the successful product of Emma's hard work—and paid no support for Emma or the children. She had to increase her horse business revenues to manage the ranch and create financial security for herself.

When the kids were at their father's, Emma worked all day and into the night. She didn't eat and became thin. She was entrapped in her own lies of what it meant to be a person of value. She kept trying to prove her worth to an unseen critic buried deep in her unconscious. But she didn't know that was what she was doing. She couldn't see that she was still on the hamster wheel and that no matter how much success she created, it was still never enough. She kept raising the bar higher and higher.

Emma spent so much time at work trying to make a living that she wasn't taking time in her garden to enjoy the flowers or pick the berries that had so delighted her. Without realizing it, she was punishing herself for breaking up the family. She judged herself for allowing her life to be dominated for so long. She tormented herself by taking away all her pleasures.

She likened herself to a workhorse: efficient, hard-working, and never tiring. She started a café with her daughter to empower her to have her own business. Emma wanted to be part of her local economy and educate people on healthy, organic food.

She didn't want to admit it, but she was still riding the people around and around—without a care for herself. Her spirit self had finally had enough of Emma's avoidance to reclaim her dignity. She did the only thing she knew to do and created a wake-up call that was sure to get Emma's attention.

Emma's routine mammogram showed abnormalities in her left breast. The oncologist gave her a choice. "You can either get a biopsy now or wait six months."

"Why would I wait six months? These abnormalities have been here for a while now, and it is clear they are getting worse. If I am going to have to get a biopsy in six months, why don't I get one now?"

"It's really up to you," he said, not listening to her.

"What would you have your wife do in this situation?"

"Probably have her wait."

Feeling that something about the oncologist's recommendation seemed "off," Emma spoke to her father. "Yes, I agree," he told her. "Why don't you wait?"

"No, I want the biopsy now," Emma felt proud inside that she stood up to these two male authority figures and took a stand for her own health.

The doctors found cancer in two areas during the biopsy and performed a partial mastectomy at the time, yet after the surgery, no one followed up with her to explain what had taken place. Emma didn't realize that she had had a partial mastectomy or had cancer until she received the biopsy report six weeks later. Emma was on her own to find an oncologist she could trust and figure out what to do next.

The energy required for her to stand up for herself, the deep shame that still lived in her bones, mixed with the emotional pain and tears she had experienced over the last three years since the end of her marriage, had finally caught up with her. Emma was stunned, even though she had felt hunted by this dis-ease for years now.

She vowed to take better care of herself. She did her own research about the type of cancer she had. She knew she had to take her health into her own hands. She focused on growing her own food with a new fervor.

Your Hand Held Out to Me This Way

Optimistic in the dark of day.
Reminding me not to stray.
Patiently waiting,
Your hand held out to me this way.

While the rug gets pulled from beneath my feet,
You stay
Sharing your smile in the dark of day.
Your heart is deep and wide
Beating with the changing tide.

When my land is on the auction block
You pray
That it will be mine for another day.

And when the evening fog sets in
You remind me to go within
And find the arrow
That cuts through the sky
That answers the question "Why?"

Even as the wind beats to and fro upon my fragile windowpane
You remind my heart to beat again,
Finding a time when all will be well and good
As you always knew it would.

Your hand held out to me this way.

Opportunities and Contemplations

REFLECTION

I was working so hard to hold onto the ranch I literally lost the forest through the trees. I thought I was attending to myself well enough. But, in truth, I was not. There was still a huge hole in my heart, and my spirit self was wounded. I was guilt-ridden from the pain the divorce caused my children. I had failed at the one most important thing in my life, to protect my children. But was that really what it was about, or was there more?

As I searched for clues, I became more and more aware of how much I was being driven by my fear of the land being taken away, as it had with my ancestors. Even though I could see what was happening internally, I still didn't know how to stop it. I couldn't stop the illusion that I could some-how repair the trauma my ancestors and even my mother experienced.

I felt the blood memory of my ancestors as a deep unspoken anxiety that at any moment, someone could come along and take everything away—my land, my life, my food, and water. I even had a recurring expe-rience of a spear piercing my back and entering my heart whenever I was in a healing session. I was being betrayed by someone I trusted—literally stabbed in the back.

It wasn't until I took a "bird's eye view" to see this memory and fear as an ancestral trauma that I was able to find a new way to make sense of my life experience. How could I take responsibility for a past that happened before I was born? Coming to the humbling realization that I could not change the past was the beginning of my personal healing.

Meanwhile, a few seasons came and went, and I began to accept my life as a single woman. Of course, when I least expected it, a new man entered my life. He was so different from my previous lovers. He was kind, generous, and loving. He became my rock and protected me in a way I had never experienced. When I got scared, like a wounded animal, he held me tightly and whispered, "I love you. It is going to be okay."

In my memory, no one had ever done that for me before. And, if they had, I didn't recognize that kind of love at that time. Now, my animal body melted into his strong embrace, and for the first time in my life, I experienced a sense of safety and calm that previously I only felt when I was alone in nature or with my horses.

We fell in love quickly and joined our lives together with a renewed sense of joy for both of us. I liked who he was as a good role model of a man for my children. That was paramount.

One month after my wedding to my new love, I was diagnosed with breast cancer for a second time. The second cancer was life-threatening. It got my attention. I knew I had to surrender to its lesson. I had to learn to respect and love myself, something I had not yet learned how to do. I had talked about it, coached others to do it, but I wasn't fully honoring my whole being.

This time, my life was at stake in a way I had not experienced before. I had not been taking care of my spirit. I had my three children and a new love, the man of my dreams I had waited my whole life to meet. I wanted to survive for them. And, just as importantly, I wanted to survive because I wanted to prove to myself that I could set my spirit free. I still had many stories of hope and redemption to tell.

Without love, there is no healing. One of my dear friend's first responses to my second diagnosis was, "You have to love yourself."

I wanted to say, "Piss off!" I knew he was right, but I really didn't want to go there. I hated that notion that I still did not love myself, but I knew it was true. I had no choice but to wrestle with my resistance to loving myself.

As difficult as it was to face, I could see that when we become too self-possessed, whether through self-damnation or outer accusations of blame and wrongful intent, we lose our medicine, our ability to heal, and our ability to be in balance. We lose our ability to be the one little drop of water that contributes to either an angry torrent that breaks down dams or sparkling drops of glory.

WITHOUT LOVE, THERE IS NO HEALING

I invite you, maybe even implore you, to love yourself no matter what. It's not a selfish task, but rather an essential task to be the woman warrioress. We need your strength and your resilience now. It doesn't matter if you or the women who came before you were downtrodden. Now is the time to rise and shine without apology.

Mother Earth needs you now. Join me in our love song, our ode to love. It starts right here right now.

- Do you love yourself?
- Make a practice several times a day to put a smile on your face and say, "I love you!" to you. Say "I love you!" to your body.
- Thank your body for carrying you around all these years and putting up with your neglect or overuse.
- Thank your spirit self for always being there, even if in the background, the one who calls attention to when you have wandered away from who you are.

TIME IN NATURE CONTEMPLATION

Go to nature: a forest, a waterway, a flower garden. Notice something you love about the place you are in. Share your love. Call in your own "I love you," spoken to yourself. Share it with the nature around you.

The Water Calls

Lush green fields, now a golden hue, swayed in the strong, unseasonal winds. Emma felt like the golden grasses were being moved by a greater being. She saw before her so many unknowns. In spite of the pressure to bend, she stood tall. She leaned toward the sky like a blade of milky oats, flush with seed.

"Thank you, Great Mother, for the comforts you provide. I call quiet into my heart. My home is inside me." Emma whispered into the grasses, affirming her place in the family of beings.

"Come to me, dear one," her spirit guides called out to her. Emma knew it was time to surrender, to let go of the fight.

"Come to me, Emma," the forest called. "It's time to let go of your hardships. It's time to find peace in your heart. Follow me; I will show you the way."

The broken woman listened. "Where can I find you?" she whispered. "I miss you so much."

"Follow your nose. You know how; just follow your nose." And with that, the forest went quiet.

Emma stopped what she was doing. She was exhausted. She reminded herself of the vision she had with Rose, as if she, too, were circling and circling—as if her life were in jeopardy. She could barely breathe.

A drive up the coast alongside the ocean might break the lock she had placed around her heart. So, she got in her red truck with her two dogs and drove up the coast. She wasn't sure where she'd end up. She trusted the right place would find her.

A few hours up the coast, after smelling the sea salt air and watching the sea lions rest on the sandy beaches below the road, she stopped. She drove up a one-lane road, where she saw a dense forest of pine and fir.

Emma went into the forest and found a spring overflowing with fresh water, creating a new stream. Many of her plant friends were there, waiting for her to join them. She took in the aromatic fragrance of the green tips on crusty old grandma trees. She said hello to the little fairies in the fern gully and said thanks to the frog who came to visit her at the edge of the spring. She sat down where the water overflowed and began its journey to the creek below.

She could hear the fresh water trickling and bouncing its way to meet the muddy, wet earth. She watched with envy as it quietly meandered past the fern gully and wild mushrooms at its mini-shores.

"You move with such ease," Emma said to the water. "You know where you are going, and you look so free. You are fluid, present, and purposeful." A wild curiosity and new enthusiasm awakened inside her. "Perhaps I can learn from you how you so easily accomplish what seems so difficult for me. Will you teach me?" Emma asked.

With that question, everything on her "to-do list," all the things she thought she knew, and all her certainties disappeared. Only the mystery of the water remained.

"Follow the water," whispered Grandmother Tree that towered over her and sheltered her from the negative energies far away. Smiley came to her side and breathed quietly into the palm of her hand. "I'm here with you, sweet girl."

Emma looked up to thank the gnarled tree, and just as she did, a little water drop fell from the bright green moss of the tree's moist trunk into the not-yet tiny stream.

More water drops fell onto Emma's maroon robe that she had donned for this occasion and rolled off to meet the other water drops. Her attention wandered as she began to hear the river far away, where the seals had their pups.

Emma closed her eyes as Grandmother Tree spoke. "The river has no beginning and no end. The drop of water from the moss on my trunk comes from the upper canopy of my leaves that comes from the rain that comes from the clouds that come from the sea. The spring in the ground comes from the earth, which comes from the rain, which comes from the clouds, which come from the sea.

"Follow the water drops as they meet the spring. See the millions of water drops gather together to meet other springs. The springs gather together to form creeks, which flow consistently downhill to meet yet other springs and creeks and streams. Along the way, old trees like me hold up their banks so the water can flow freely to return to the ocean of their beginning."

"I am free like the water drop," Emma said. Keeping her eyes closed, she put her tanned hand on the moss of Grandmother Tree. She could feel the moist bright green elegance and how the moss moved water.

"I am water." Emma whispered. "I shall go with you."

Without another thought, she became the water drop falling from the wet moss of Grandmother Tree. The medicine of the water filled her blood with movement. She allowed herself to join the other water beings, and she started to float down the spring's fluid path. She was tossed along ever so gently as she met other springs. The water grew bigger, its momentum quicker as it moved without hesitation toward its destination.

Emma heard whales in the distance welcoming her pending arrival. She felt no resistance as the waters accelerated faster and plowed around fallen trees and branches. Fish swam beside her and splashed her a smile before they darted off. She trusted the river to carry her to the sea. Her "one-water-drop self" buoyantly and gracefully dodged rocks as they tried to change her course.

As the waters neared the sea, Emma saw people standing by the shores of the now muddy river, full of fallen trees and a stray boat here and there. The people were angry. They were yelling at people on the other side of the river. Both sides were pointing fingers and hurling profanities at each other across the river's width. Their words fell into the river like poison daggers breaking her symmetry. The waters became muddier and full of silt.

The people on either side of the river were so focused on the opposite side that they didn't notice the river was getting bigger and fiercer. Her anger grew as the people on both shores continued to shout and blame each other. The people didn't notice that the soils under their feet were falling into the river, and they were losing ground. The river was tempted to take a few people in her embrace as she tried to get their attention.

Emma was upset. She wished the people would stop. "Can't you see this amazing river before you? Can't you feel the forest beside you? Instead, you blame others. *I am not you. I am water, and I belong to the sea.*"

Just then, she saw her friend, a woman who had lost her husband and was struggling with breast cancer, crying tears into the river. She was judging herself for not being good enough. She saw the pained woman's tears transform into free-spirit water balls of energy. The river had taken them and shifted their shape.

Emma wanted to help her, but she could not. The river was moving too fast. The river heard Emma's cry and felt her outstretched hand, and she said quietly under her watery breath, "You only have yourself to save now. Focus on your freedom. Call in your new home of belonging. Don't distract yourself with the pain of others now. They each have their own destiny, and you cannot control that."

The waters gurgled and swept her swiftly to the sea, where she swam with the seals like she had done so many times in her imagination as a girl. She dove into the salty water, surfacing, rolling, and heading under again with a tap of her tail on the water's surface as if to send a splash of new water molecules up into the air to be carried to faraway places.

A Woman Standing

A woman standing
In cowgirl's clothes,
Hat on mane,
Boots on tender toes.

She is the image of strength and hope,
With babies one and two in hand
And baby three, atop her hip, she stands.
Baby three's hand upon her breast as if to fortify all the rest.
A mother and her babes, a tangled knot of love engaged.

She gives me strength, she does
And even reminds me of a few
Women I know, just like you.
Full of love and fierceness
All in one
Don't mess with her
Or you'll surely come undone.

Like a lioness with her cubs, she glows
And gives me strength and love, you know.

Opportunities and Contemplations

REFLECTION

A number of authors reveal a growing understanding that some people who are highly empathic, and even telepathic, are mediators between the human world and nature. When I read David Abrams, *The Spell of The Sensuous*, I felt like I was being seen for who I am for the first time in my life—in actuality, I was seeing myself clearly for the first time. I could see that I was a medicine person, a shaman, someone who is not defined by boundaries of a particular culture or social customs. Instead, just as he describes, my first allegiance is to the earthly web of relations and secondarily to the human community. This knowing helped me return to my spirit self.

I missed the forests and the creeks of my youth. When the plant world started to call to me, it seemed meant to be. I found a forest homeland where I could rest and heal in Point Arena. My new love and I stayed there for three years. I went into the forest daily and took lessons from the trees. I studied the wild medicinal plants all around me that I had ignored for so long. I meandered on the beaches, collecting shells and seaweed. I planted a new garden and many fruit trees.

My children had grown up and were out of the house, living their own journeys. They were what my life had been all about, and I missed them. But now, it was my time to discover who I was to become. My children, too, needed to find their freedom and unique paths in life.

Nature and all my plant and animal friends remind me of my freedom every day. They invite me to run and skip, to laugh and love. My heart grew open again.

During my time in the forest, I learned to forgive. Forgiveness is shown to reduce depression and anxiety and improve feelings of hope. In Latin, forgive means to give before. To give doesn't mean to forget. It doesn't mean to let someone off the hook, so to speak. It means to relax the hurt around your heart; to stop holding on to the pain of the past. To not make their story yours.

I spent time forgiving my mother. I practiced the Ho☒oponopono prayer that goes something like this:

I am sorry

I love you,

Please forgive me,

Thank you.

Each morning, I first said it to my mother, then to Mother Earth, and then to myself. It was powerful. I still do it to this day.

Through this life-transforming healing, the world I surround myself in today allows me to finally give myself permission to be unapologetically me. I am a woman of nature. I know I am always loved when I am in nature. And I can now give my love freely without being abused.

YOU ARE A CHILD OF MOTHER EARTH

Mother Earth needs you now. Join me in a love song or ode to love—it starts right here right now.

- Who do you need to forgive?
- It is okay to forgive yourself. Try that on. I highly recommend it.
- Practice the Ho'oponopono. There is no right place to start. You can start with yourself, with someone who has hurt you, someone you love, or someone you want to make peace with.

I am sorry

I love you,

Please forgive me,
Thank you.

- Is there a community or group of people you feel compelled to help, to nurture? What is one simple statement you want to embody when you hold the space for them?

TIME IN NATURE CONTEMPLATION

Go to nature: a forest, a waterway, a flower garden. Notice something you love about the place you are in. Share your love. Be your own story, speaking "I love you" to yourself. Share it with the nature around you. Notice what makes you smile and feel happy. Let yourself be free. It's time.

Call in the "free you." Call out to all the plants and animals, "I am!" No apologies. Yell out loud for all of nature to hear: *"I am Free! I am Free!"*

What Was Lost Is Found

Years passed before Emma returned from her time in the forest and frolicking at sea. She was finally ready for her new life. She didn't know what that meant or how it would look. But she felt ready. She was reconnected to her spirit self, and she trusted that when the time was right, a message would arrive from somewhere to guide her to her new home of belonging.

She sat down to do her daily emails and, oddly, a photo of a ranch with a log house filled her computer screen. Without a second thought, she opened the email and was quite taken with pictures of this ranch. It had been for sale for over four years.

The ranch looked shockingly familiar. She had to go see it. And see it, she did. She drove down a winding, one-lane road studded with forest and full of aromatic fragrances. The road followed a creek that meandered to the sea, as all creeks do. The sensations that ran through her were familiar. It reminded her of the roads she walked every day and the creeks she played in as a girl.

The entrance to the ranch was a solid wooden bridge that crossed a year-round creek. It then wound past an ancient apple orchard, only to meander once again along the creek. Just as she wondered if she was in the right place, the simple log cabin appeared, surrounded by flowering rhododendrons. Sharp green leaves and full-blossomed red flowers announced her arrival.

The realtor showed Emma and her beloved around the ranch. They went up to the top to see the pastoral elegance overlooking the ocean and walked back down through fern gullies and ancient groves of redwoods that had survived deforestation. The bay trees, buckeye, and even the coyote brush waved to welcome her. It reminded her of her childhood home.

As Emma and her man, her solid rock who had stood by her through her breast cancer and her deep transformation, prepared to leave, the realtor asked, "Well, what do you think?"

Without a moment's hesitation, her other half spoke confidently, "Let's make an offer." Emma looked at him, surprised. He was usually quite soft-spoken. His sureness matched hers, and she gleefully replied, "Yes, indeed!"

And so, after all her trials and errors, her wishes indeed came true. One thing led to another and, before she knew it, she was unpacking in her new home. She felt grounded and settled in these familiar surroundings as if she had never left. She was far enough away from the city of people but close enough for her children to visit back and forth. She pinched herself just to make sure it was real.

As she thumbed through one of her medicinal herb books that had sat on the bookshelf unattended for too many years, a paper fell out from between the abandoned pages. It was a school paper with its perfectly proportioned blue lines running across the page so students could write uniformly on a straight line.

She recognized her own handwriting. It was a seventh-grade assignment to write about your "dream home." The world stopped as she sat down to read it:

"I would like a little cottage with a loft as a second floor. The first floor would have a living room, kitchen, hall, and bathroom. The house would be in the midst of a vast valley. I would have many acres of rolling land for horses and stock to roam.

"By my home, there is a creek. There would be many trees covering the house and the area. I would like a swimming pool with a stable behind it. Five stalls would be fine, and a corral with a bunch of other pastures for foals and goats and such. Behind the stalls would be a hay barn and tie stalls for when it was storming. A tack room would be in front of the stalls, closer to the house, where I keep my grain and tack. There would be a garden in the back of my house, a little way from my pool. That is the house I want."

Emma looked up to the top right of the page and noted that the teacher had given her a B- for her paper. "Your grade would have been better if a floor plan of your house had been handed in," the teacher wrote.

Emma broke out in a deep belly laugh. She *had* written about her house. Her home was mostly outside. That's what had been important to her for as long as she could remember. She recalled wishing for a ranch of her own someday—a piece of dirt that could never be taken away and a place where she could share her love with her community of plants and animals and relish in the glory of nature.

And then she laughed again and indignantly replied to the teacher as if she were sitting next to her. "How dare you grade my dream! How dare you give me a B- because your idea of a house is how many rooms it has and what colors you paint the walls. How dare you try to squash my spirit girl's dream!"

She thought about how her teacher's narrow perspective may have shaped her into the silent gun barrel of what and who she should be as a girl. She thought about all the other subtle, but profound, messages she had received since before she could even remember. They no longer had a place in her thoughts. And certainly not in her house.

Emma framed her little girl's description of her dream home and put it on the wall of her studio so she would never again forget who she was and how she wanted to live. It didn't matter what anyone else thought.

She now had the wisdom to turn away from deception. And without another thought, she stepped outside of her little log cabin, strode up the steep hill to the top of the pastoral wonderland where her horses were free.

Emma was a woman of nature, never to be tamed. She was now wild and free, despite others' opinions or attempts to keep her locked inside a stall.

She was Keoki's great-granddaughter. She was Lilian and Lucy's granddaughter. She was Nancy's daughter. She had broken the tragedies of the women before her. Her daughters were free to be empowered women. Her son was free to marry an empowered woman.

Emma smiled at the sun as the colors of the sky turned orange and then red. The horses circled around her, quietly sharing the sacred space they had each created. The sun touched the sea's dark horizon and blew Emma a kiss on the salty pearls of mist. "Welcome home, dear one."

Thank You

An hour before dawn,
The bottom of the sky begins to sparkle
As it meets the rolling hilltops
Turning a lighter shade of night.
The morning mist tickles my face
As it enters my open window.

I am out of bed, Earl Grey steeping in the teapot.
The deep orange sliver of morning
Spans the pastoral horizon
Sandwiched between the black silhouette of the land
And the dark blue of the now starless sky.

As I ponder how such diverse colors
Can blend together to make a morning,
I catch the dark shape of an owl right in front of me
As if she has been waiting for me all this time.

She reminds me to enjoy reverently
This quiet moment before dawn.
Together we fill our lungs with air
And consider what it means
To transform night into day.

"I am the guardian of the night," she says,
"And you are the guardian of the day."
A private moment of gratitude passes between us.
And just as I imagine it is time for her to fill her belly
With the last mouse of the night
She lifts off the branches of the small pine tree.

And so, I begin my day, knowing that the land will hold me up
As long as I listen to her gifts and respect her magic.
And I say, "Thank you."

ARIANA

I Send My Love to You

Thank you for sharing my journey and for sharing yours. Never forget that you are supported by the wonders of nature, ready for your attention. Allow, listen, explore, and remove judgment from your daily routine. You are divine, beautiful, and amazing!

Welcome Home!

ACKNOWLEDGMENTS

Firstand most importantly, I want to thank my children for choosing me to be their mom, for loving me in spite of my humanness, and for teaching me life lessons from each of their unique perspectives. I want to thank my mom for always having animals in the house and my father for his wisdom, his imaginative artistry, and for taking us into nature. My husband, Casey, deserves special gratitude for his patience and love over the many years it took me to write this book and the range of emotions it brought out in me as I re-opened old wounds to find my personal resolution.

I want to thank the Great Spirit and Mother Earth for asking me to try to bring voice to the wonders beyond logical reason and to build a bridge between the human world and the natural world. Important people in my life include Terry Schultz, my raptor teacher who taught me how to be a leader; my junior high school teacher, Mrs. Burleson, who let me draw pictures on my desk instead of reading in class; Mr. Phillips, a retired farmer who handed me *National Wildlife* magazines over the fence when he caught me peering into his garden; to Mimi, my other neighbor who taught me how to make pie when she found me sneaking around her gardens; and to one of my early riding teachers, Peggy Adams, who was part of the earth in human form.

The Water Calls and my dignity would not be here if it was not for my first horse, Sumi, my greatest friend and teacher, and for RT17 and all the owls, eagles, and hawks who let me hold them next to my heart as we intimately healed each other's wounds. And of course to Raven who forced me to look in the mirror, Coyote who showed me how to set myself free, and to my sheep for all the range of emotions I have gleaned from caring for them—laughing, crying, guiding, loving—and especially to their wool that keeps me warm at night as I dream.

I honor the water that takes my tears and transforms them into the intricate web of life—to the creek, the estuary, the ocean, the rain and snow—all moving within and through me, holding me and reminding me to love, to forgive, to honor, and to cherish every moment of my life.

A special thanks to Wendy Norris and Susan Hagen who edited my first drafts of the book and offered creative prompts to encourage me to dig deeper. And then, Donna Mazzitelli, the book's final editor and publisher who nudged me even more to share my most vulnerable feelings, allowing me to complete *The Water Calls* with a new sense of dignity and freedom I would not have found without her caring support.

I'd also like to thank my friends Kathleen McCauley Anast, Hallie Bigliardi, Amanda Komiko Kent, Ashley Smith, Kansas Carradine, and Sue Tucker for loving me through thick and thin, who supported me when I fell down, and for being there with a smiling face as I learned once again to stand tall without apology.

Words cannot convey the depth of honor and sacred relationship to the horses in my life who have taught me to share my love with people, to let go of fear and judgment, to trust my intuition, to stand my ground, and to know that my feelings are real and I am a good person worthy of love and respect.

ABOUT THE AUTHOR

Ariana Strozzi Mazzucchi grew up on the back of a horse on the coastal hills of Northern California. She enjoys sharing her love of animals, land, and nature with anyone who crosses her path. Her mission is to reconnect people to the natural world for the sake of saving the Great Mother Earth and all her creations.

She believes that time is of the essence. We need to take the reins in our own hands, form herds of like-minded people, share our dreams, and stand tall in the face of adversity. We need to awaken our spiritual longing and interconnectedness to all life and encourage possibility and hope in a time of uncertainty.

Ariana is a pioneer in the field of incorporating horses into human education and learning, coining the term equine-guided education (EGE) in 1999. She began pioneering this work in the 1970s, training horse and rider in a variety of disciplines and winning champion awards in dressage, jumping, eventing, gymkhana, reining, and working cow horse.

During this time, she realized that horses were listening to subtle forms of energy, intention, and imagery. She believes she grew up knowing this, but her consciousness expanded immensely once she brought it into cognitive form. She began to see people as animals also and went on to study animal behavior at UC Davis, where she graduated with a degree in zoology in 1984.

Ariana spent several years working with birds of prey and other wildlife at the UC Davis Veterinary School and managed several animal and equine facilities. The birds and wildlife taught her many of the same lessons that the horses had. She felt a need to bring the magic of animal communication into the world of people and began studying human dynamics—aikido, leadership, and somatics—becoming a Master Somatic Coach in 1996.

The seemingly separate worlds of horsemanship and self-mastery began to blend together and ultimately shifted her orientation from traditional horsemanship (in which we control the horse's behavior through a system of cues and orders) to seeing the horse as a sentient being who can actually guide us into a deeper connection with ourselves and our whole lives.

She started to bring people out to work with the horses, not to learn how to work or ride the horse, but to practice energy awareness and centering. It was then she realized that the horses gave each person a truly unique experience that directly related to every other area of his or her life. This led to the beginning of Leadership & Horses™ in 1989.

Ariana's students come from all walks of life, including youth, mothers, coaches, therapists, managers, small business owners, entrepreneurs, and corporate executives. Horses and the natural world have taught her to become more curious about helping people find their own reconnection to the natural world so they can come back into balance in their lives and have a better chance of staying on their destiny's path.

She learned that the healing power of land and animals is profound beyond measure and also learned that our path is right in front of us once we get out of our clogged, logical appeals and rationalizations. Finally, she learned that it takes time to slough off and let go of the deeper underlying stories and experiences that stop us from being free in spirit and purpose.

Ariana Strozzi Mazzucchi is the author of the books, *Equine Guided Education: Horses Healing Humans, Healing Earth; Horse Sense for the Leader Within; Planning Your Business in the "Horse as Healer/Teacher" Professions*, and the DVD *Intuitive Horsemanship*™, as well as essays in the books, *Being Human at Work* and *Horse Crazy*. She cofounded the Strozzi Institute and has been in numerous agricultural board of director positions.

In addition to her love of horses, Ariana is an avid rancher, plant medicine grower, winemaker, artist, and mother of three. As an artist, she loves to work in a variety of mediums, including scratchboard, sumi painting, oils, acrylics, beadwork, and watercolor.

To learn more about Ariana, visit ArianaStrozziMazzucchi.com.

INVITE ARIANA TO YOUR BOOK CLUB!

As a special gift to readers of *The Water Calls,* Ariana would love to visit your book club either via video conferencing or in person. Please contact Ariana directly to schedule her appearance at your next book club meeting. arianamazzucchi@gmail.com.

STAY CONNECTED!

To stay connected, please be sure to find Ariana online at https://www.facebook.com/ariana.strozzimazzucchi/

You can also visit her website: ArianaStrozziMazzucchi. com or drop her a line at arianamazzucchi@gmail.com.

And one last favor ...

If you have been touched by *The Water Calls,* please be sure to visit her Goodreads, Barnes & Noble, and Amazon book pages and leave a review.

Thank you!

ABOUT THE PRESS

Merry Dissonance Press is a hybrid indie publisher/book producer of works of transformation, inspiration, exploration, and illumination. MDP takes a holistic approach to bring books into the world that make a little noise and create dissonance within the whole so ALL can be resolved to produce beautiful harmonies.

Merry Dissonance Press works with its authors every step of the way to craft the finest books and help promote them. Dedicated to publishing award-winning books, we strive to support talented writers and assist them to discover, claim, and refine their distinct voices. Merry Dissonance Press is the place where collaboration and facilitation of our shared human experiences join together to make a difference in our world.

For more information, visit merrydissonancepress.com.